The Masters of the Spirit

A GOLF FABLE

Anne Kinsman Fisher

HarperSanFrancisco
An Imprint of HarperCollins*Publishers*

This story is a work of fiction. The references to real people
(living or dead) and historical events are intended solely to
lend the fiction its proper historical context.

FIRST EDITION

Library of Congress Cataloging-in-Publication Data
Fisher, Anne Kinsman
The masters of the spirit : a golf fable / Anne Kinsman Fisher. —1st ed.
ISBN 0-06-251471-7 (cloth)
1. Golfers—Fiction. I. Title.
PS3556.I7948M3   1997
813'.54—dc21   96-49047

97 98 99 00 01 ❖ RRDH 10 9 8 7 6 5 4 3 2 1

Contents

THERE IS A PLACE IN EVERY GOLFER'S IMAGINATION, a place where the sacred converges with living experience. It is neither heaven nor earth, but a cathedral of nature placed, inexplicably, somewhere in between.

The sun always shines low on this golf course, filtered by the morning mist. The grass is always dusted with a layer of dew, and the greens are always freshly cut. It is here that you are beyond worry, in a serene, idyllic place suspended in timelessness.

Here you break through the barriers life has put between you and your dreams, and the best in you is brought forth.

To the greatest golfer in the world:
my father, Bob Thomas

Acknowledgments

A SPECIAL THANKS TO MY EDITOR, Lisa Bach, who first inspired this book, and to the incomparable team at Harper San Francisco for excellence and enthusiasm that go way beyond the call of duty: Mike Leonard, Tom Grady, Margery Buchanan, and Kathy Reigstad.

I also want to thank:

My family, whose support has been immeasurable: my mother, agent, editor, and best friend, Mary Anne Thomas; both of my beloved fathers, Robert Kinsman Fisher and Bob Thomas; and my brother, Jeffrey.

Janet Mills, my treasured friend and publisher, who selflessly supported this book and allowed it to fly.

Don Horak, Albert Stoddard, and Mary Rose Busby, two southern gentlemen and a gentlewoman in the tradition of Bobby Jones.

And my prayer circle, whose lavish attention nurtured me through the writing of this book: Suzan and Joseph Woods (a special thanks for naming West Wind); Karen Bouvier; the Reverend Margee Grounds, and my spiritual family at Unity of Savannah.

Prologue

WHEN SHE WAS A LITTLE GIRL, I lulled her to sleep with golf stories instead of fairy tales. I hoped that somehow golf would help her find herself and that it would show her the one reason she was on this earth.

I told her it was possible to come back from almost certain death as we relived Ben Hogan's 1950 victory at the U.S. Open at Merion. I dropped hints about the one-iron that had mysteriously disappeared from Hogan's bag that day, hoping she would join in my search for it at Saturday morning yard sales. Who knows when greatness will make another appearance? I explained.

You can find love as a golfer, I told her, and recounted the day Bobby Jones returned to St. Andrews, Scotland, after a trip to the 1936 Berlin Olympics. Stopping there to play a casual round of golf on his way home to Augusta, Jones thought his outing ruined when he spotted thousands of people crowding the course. They must be holding a tournament, he thought. My daughter's favorite part of the tale always came when I said, "Nope, there was no tournament. The crowds were there for him. Word had spread when he called for a tee time. 'Bobby's back,' the townspeople had whispered to each other. 'Bobby's back.'"

When other little girls were begging for stories about the three bears, my daughter was saying, "Tell me one more time, Daddy, how Bobby came back."

She's no longer a little girl. Today she's a grown woman, lying in a hospital bed. And I'm not her strong and handsome father anymore. My shoulders are slumped from worry. My hair, no longer blond, shines silver in the fluorescent hospital lighting. I feel like an old man, impotent and alone.

As I pick up her unresponsive hand, I find I can't stop myself from crying. I make no attempt to wipe away the tears; they flow unchecked down the wrinkles on my face.

"I have a tumor, Daddy," she told me only a week ago. "A small lump in my breast that won't go away."

Now she's lying in a hospital bed, still anesthetized and lifeless after her surgery. I'm waiting for the results of the biopsy, waiting to find out if my daughter has cancer. She looks so thin and helpless, her dark hair splayed against the sterile white pillowcase, but she still has a light around her, and so I cling to the hope that she'll be all right.

I taught her everything I know about life: how to stand up to its challenges with courage, grace, and gentleness. Now I desperately hope it's been enough. I couldn't bear to lose her.

Her hand softly squeezes my own, and I know she's waking up. I'm glad, because I have a story to tell her. A golf story. I should have told her this one a long time ago, and I chide myself mercilessly for keeping silent. It's a true story about a very unusual round of golf I played about twenty years ago. At the time, I thought what I learned on that golf course was meant for me alone. Now, looking at my daughter's pale face, I know I was wrong. My story is for all people struggling to find their way on the course of life.

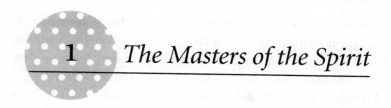

1 The Masters of the Spirit

Twenty years ago, in 1976, I stumbled onto a velvety green golf course mythically carved out of the Wasatch Mountains and met my hero, Bobby Jones. He was playing with seven of his friends. Altogether, they were eight of the greatest champions the game had ever seen. I was so dumbfounded in the presence of these masters that I forgot Bobby Jones had been dead since 1971.

It was a private tournament, an annual rite of spiritual mastery that transcended logic and reason. Each man had a secret that enabled him, year after year, even long after death, to gather with the others in this hallowed cathedral of golf, hidden within the red desert mountains of Utah. These secrets had enabled each of them to reach the pinnacle of championship golf, to play to near perfection.

I shall try to explain the mystery to you, revealing the secrets exactly as I learned them.

It was a newly minted spring morning when I found them there, assembled for their annual game. The day was April 14, 1976. It was a coincidence that I happened to find them on that Rocky Mountain golf course. If you believe in coincidences.

My name is Zachary Tobias, and I'm a salesman. Well, technically speaking, I'm a sales *trainer,* for my days as a journeyman traveling from customer to customer are long past. Now I teach my craft to younger men, but I still like being called a salesman. Perhaps I'm old-fashioned that way. I believe that sales is an art, that what I do—what I've always done—is see into someone's heart and give that person what he or she most desires.

This is why I've always loved golf. Golf is an intimate sport. Each shot, whether good or bad, is a conversation between the golfer and the course. When I play golf, I envision the heart of the course, much the same way I see into the hearts of my clients. In this way, the two great passions of my life are joined.

I remember arriving in Salt Lake City that long-ago April morning. The city was a basin of fog, surrounded by the desert mountains. The craggy, still-snowcapped peaks were unfamiliar to me. I'd never been in the West before; it wasn't my territory. But this April I'd been asked to call on a newly opened chain of drugstores throughout the Rocky Mountain states. Utah was my first stop.

As my plane descended into the valley city, I scanned the ground for a golf course. I'd just rediscovered the game after a long absence.

When I was young, golf had been taken away from me. Back then, I was the star of my high school golf team and had won the city championship three years in a row. My final victory was in 1963. I was offered a full golf scholarship to the University of Texas. Even today I wonder what my life would have been like had I taken that scholarship. Would I have won the NCAA tournament? Would I have become a tour player, perhaps even a champion?

I'll never know. My parents insisted that I enroll at Pennsylvania State University instead and study engineering, so that I'd have a solid education to fall back on. I was horribly out of place at Penn State, my talent for communication lost amongst the brainy math majors of the engineering department. I left Penn State, and my dreams of golf, after the first semester.

Oddly, it was my love for sales that brought me back to golf. A client invited me to play with him, and as soon as I smelled the sweet, loamy scent of freshly cut grass and felt the slippery dew under my feet, I knew I'd come home.

My plane landed in Utah in the early afternoon. After checking into my hotel, I headed for the lounge, where I borrowed a phone book in which to search for a course. Perhaps I'd looked long enough for my dreams that, at last, the golfing gods smiled upon me. Or perhaps I simply fell through a crack in time, into the magic of the game.

Either way, my adventure began.

"Have you found the course you're looking for?"

I jumped slightly, startled by the voice. It belonged to a man sitting on the barstool next to mine.

He pointed to the phone book I'd been looking through. "Aren't you looking for a golf course?"

"Yes," I said. "This is my first trip out West, and I'm hoping the mountain air will improve my game a little. Are you familiar with the courses here?"

"I'm familiar with the reasons men play golf," he answered.

There was something about his words that cut to my heart, as if he knew more about my life than I did, and I looked at him more closely. He was perhaps sixty years old, his face broad and tanned, with distinctive sloping planes. His skin wasn't wrinkled, though, and for an instant he looked like a young man.

"Zachary Tobias," I said, extending my hand.

"Ben Nighthorse."

"Do you play golf?"

"My people have always played golf." He chose his words with deliberateness.

"Really?" I questioned. "But you know that golf was invented in Scotland."

He chuckled softly, almost as if he were rebuking me.

"Have you found the course you're looking for?" he persisted, pointing at the phone book once again.

"Not yet. So far, I've ruled out the city courses," I explained. "They'll be too crowded. I like to play alone, just myself and my game. Can you recommend one?" I added as an afterthought.

He waited a few seconds before replying, the pause hanging palpably in the air. When he finally spoke again, his words were careful and measured. "Each golfer has his own journey to follow. I must know what you're looking for before I can recommend a course. Tell me about yourself."

A golfer has his own journey to follow? I wasn't quite sure what my journey was, but I started to tell the old man about my life, hoping to find out. I wasn't unhappy, not at all. I loved my job; it was the accompanying corporate politics I hated. I enjoyed traveling, but I ached with loneliness whenever I was separated from my family. I didn't like the compromises required of me, but I'd made my peace with them. What bothered me was a nagging suspicion that my life had another purpose, that I had unfulfilled dreams I didn't even know about.

"You must play West Wind," he declared.

He withdrew a pen from an inside pocket of his denim jacket and began to scribble directions on a sweaty cocktail napkin. He passed it to me, and I flipped the pages of the phone book to search for the course's number. There was no listing, and when I turned back to ask Nighthorse if he had the number, he was gone.

THE NEXT MORNING, I took the highway south as he had instructed. Even today, twenty years later, I remember each mile of the journey as if it were yesterday.

About an hour outside of Salt Lake City, I found myself on a serpentine single-lane highway that wound through a cleft in the mountains. Dry red rock rose above me, and I wondered as I passed between the sheets of earth how a golf course could be coaxed from such parched, desolate land.

After another thirty minutes, I saw a weathered sign to the left that read *West Wind Golf Club.* I turned onto the dirt road and began to climb the mountain. It was eight-thirty, and the sun was gentle, streaming across the narrow mountain road.

I saw the turnoff for the course and pulled into the parking lot. There were two cars there: a late-model Cadillac carefully polished to a dignified gleam, and a brilliant cherry-red 1955 Porsche convertible. I wondered if the drivers' personalities matched their automobiles. Was one of them quietly affluent, the other flamboyant and fun-loving?

I'd brought my favorite clubs on this trip, a vintage set of Ben Hogan Personal Model clubs made in 1954, the exact model Hogan had used during his famous triple-crown year of 1953. My set was one of the first ones ever manufactured by the Hogan Company. They were a little old-fashioned now, cutting too far into the ground if I swung too steeply, but I still loved to play with them. They made me feel like a champion.

I pulled the clubs from my car and walked toward the pro shop.

"Do you have room for a single today?" I asked the starter.

"No, I'm sorry," he replied. "I've got a private group teeing off at nine-thirty. They've booked the course for the entire day."

I must have looked crestfallen, because the starter twisted his face in sympathy, then in concentration. After a minute or two, he added, "If you tee off now, you can probably get a few holes ahead of them, and if you play quickly, they'll never know you're there."

I smiled broadly and opened my wallet, but he waved me away.

"Enjoy the round," he said.

I USUALLY WARM UP on the driving range before I start to play. I'm methodical that way. I hit three or four balls with each of my clubs. It takes a long time—sometimes nearly an hour—but I always play better because of it. It's not so much the physical practice as the mental discipline that helps. Handling each club, precisely and deliberately, reminds me that I control the outcome of the round to come.

This morning, though, I couldn't spare the time, so I went straight to the first tee. From the box, I could see the driving range off to my right. There was a lone figure there, aggressively hitting ball after ball. Dressed in fluid khaki pants, a V-neck sweater, and a flat-billed linen cap, the man looked familiar to me, but I couldn't quite place him.

I turned back to the tee and, looking downward, placed my ball.

When I glanced up again and took a good look at my surroundings, the view of the course was so magnificent that my breath caught in my throat.

The course curved around the edge of the mountain. The entire valley was laid out below like a Lilliputian village. Tiny houses separated by groves of miniature trees dotted the canyon. Other mountains rose in the distance, tall and wise, frosted with spring snow.

I took a sharp breath, and the course began to speak its magic to me.

The first hole lay before me, a par four bounded by evergreens. In shafts of mystical light, the sun streamed through the trees. I felt the hush of the course surround me, wash over me. I slid my driver from my bag with confidence. I suddenly felt that there was nothing I couldn't do. It was a feeling of awesome power.

I addressed the ball, and without even a waggle, I swung and hit a perfect drive 250 yards. I thought of nothing but the connection between me and the course. The sun lighted my path as I followed my ball up the fairway.

A large bunker, steeply faced and cut deep into the gentle upslope, protected the approach to the green. There were strange fingertips to the bunker, making it look like a Native American rendering of a bear claw. The cup was cut dangerously close to the bunker, but I decided to be bold and go for the pin.

My iron shot lofted the ball high into the air and dropped it onto the edge of the green, neatly placing it between the bunker and the pin.

I slid my putter from my bag, stroked the ball, and watched calmly as it rolled toward the pin, just slightly off to the left. As the ball neared the cup, however, it broke, curved right, and dropped in with a soft clunk. A birdie.

I moved slowly, as if in a dream, the slight westerly breeze caressing my cheek. When I finally looked back toward the tee box, I saw that I was no longer alone. There were two men standing there, filmy and transparent in the bright morning sun.

The first was the same slender man I'd seen on the driving range, his flat-billed cap pulled low to shield his eyes from the sun. The second man had a more solid build. He was dressed in a strangely old-fashioned manner: he wore softly billowing plus fours, a white shirt that looked starched even in the distance, and a tie. The first man pointed at me, and the other nodded in acknowledgment.

I walked toward them, my feet bidden by a greater power. As I approached, the hair on my arms pricked like needles.

Before me stood Ben Hogan and Bobby Jones.

JONES SPOKE FIRST. "That was a beautiful hole you played. We were just appreciating your skill." His voice was melodious, aristocratically southern. He spoke precisely, as if measuring each word for respect.

I stood staring, completely mesmerized.

Hogan broke the silence. "How did you get here?" he barked.

"W . . . well," I stammered, "I came up the mountain, looked for the dirt road—"

"That's not what I meant," he said sharply. "This is a private match. Private."

"Now, Ben," Jones chided softly. "Don't scare him off. He's the only one, in all these years, who's found us. Don't you think there may be a reason he's here?"

"Harrumph," Hogan growled.

Jones simply laughed.

Where Hogan was gruff, Jones was a gentleman. He leaned toward me and said, "What Ben meant to say is that this is a very special place. You had to *do* something to get here. What did you do?"

I stood quietly, bewildered. All I could think about was my route up the mountain.

Jones spoke again. "You must have done something that was rather like a prayer."

My heart flooded with emotion. I'd never talked about these things to anyone, but somehow, standing there before the legendary Bobby Jones, I suddenly wanted to tell him everything. How golf was sacred to me, like a walking prayer. How my heart soared with an almost religious fervor when I drove a golf ball and saw it rise in the distance.

"Heaven," I said, shifting from thoughts to words. "It was how the course looked this morning. Like a cathedral."

"Ohhhh." Jones smiled in response. "Unity. You felt the union between yourself and nature. The force that causes the grass to grow also beats in your heart. You felt it, and here you are."

Jones looked at Hogan, his eyebrows raised. "But what does it mean?" he asked softly.

"Who cares?" Hogan snorted.

Jones laughed again.

"I had a tough day all my life," Hogan blurted. "Nobody ever explained anything to me."

"But if he's found us, there must be a reason."

"*Found* you?" I interjected.

"Found us, found the course." Hogan tapped out his words in a staccato rhythm.

"I think you all call it 'the zone' nowadays," Jones added softly.

"The zone?" I exclaimed.

Hogan burst into laughter.

"Yes," Jones said. "The zone. The place where the best within you is brought forth. When you play in the zone, you shoot perfect golf—as you did on this last hole. The zone is beyond worry, beyond frustration. It's the nirvana every golfer seeks."

I realized my mouth was hanging open. I closed it and tried to regain a bit of composure. Any semblance of calm, however, eluded me. My hero, winner of the fabled Grand Slam, the ultimate master of golf, was standing before me telling me that I was in the zone.

"It's okay," Jones said softly. "We came here the same way you did—through the zone."

"But how?" I stammered.

Jones squeezed my shoulder in comfort. "It's our love for this game, in all its mythical power, that brings us back."

And then he told me about the tournament.

IT BEGAN AS AN ANNUAL MATCH between eight golfers: Walter Hagen, Byron Nelson, Ben Hogan, Arnold Palmer, Tony Lema, Jack Nicklaus, Gary Player, and Bobby Jones. It had started in 1963, at Jones's request, when they were all alive. It was a final test of champions. It was old versus young, hickory versus steel.

No one but the eight invitees knew about the tournament. They played without fans, honor among competitors being the only trophy.

Each of the eight golfers eagerly looked forward to this tournament each year, for although they were of vastly differing ages, they shared a great love for the game. These eight had a connection beyond friendship. They were compatriots. They understood and respected each other's challenges; they reveled in each other's accomplishments. The competition was fierce, don't misunderstand; but there was a richness of relationship among the eight men.

"In 1966, three years after the tournament began," Jones explained, "Tony Lema was killed. The remaining seven of us assembled here the next year in honor of Tony. Somewhere in the morning light that streamed through the trees, the mist seemed to congeal"—Jones's voice quavered at the memory—"and our friend Tony, six months after his death, walked toward us, laughing and joking as he always had, with his clubs slung over his shoulder.

"So from 1966 on," Jones continued, "all eight of us were expected to show up. Death was no excuse."

"But *how?*" I whispered, incredulous.

"Each of us has a secret," Jones replied, "a spiritual secret that empowers us to reach our ultimate skill level. That secret allows us to reach the zone, and to play here at West Wind in perpetuity.

"Perhaps the time has come," he mused, "to share our secrets with others. I've always known golf is the way to uncover great spiritual truths. Perhaps the world is hungry for what we know. Perhaps that's why you're here—to be the messenger."

My skin tingled as Jones pondered my destiny. When he turned back to me, he was resolute. "Play with us today," he invited. "We'll tell you all about it."

2 *The Secret of Chaos*

'd always known there was a secret to golf. After all, what distinguishes the great champions, if not a secret way of playing? Ben Hogan was the only one who'd been honest enough to admit it when he was alive. But now it was confirmed: they *all* had a secret.

"It's not only a secret to golf," Bobby Jones told me. "It's a secret to life." His blue eyes twinkled knowingly.

"Golf is a metaphor for life. The golf course is where, against all odds, we struggle to see—to truly *see*—the magnificence of the human spirit. And so it is in life. The challenges we face on the golf course teach us how to overcome parallel challenges in life."

As I watched him, I remembered how he'd looked in the late sixties when he'd presided over the Masters. Then he'd been confined to a wheelchair, his legs twisted with disease. Now he stood straight and unblemished before me, and I knew he spoke the truth.

Golf was life. The barriers to a perfect game were also the barriers to my dreams. I wanted to know how to conquer those barriers. More than that, I *had* to know. It was what had drawn me back to the golf course.

The three of us stood at the first tee, the silence of the course enveloping us. Hogan had pulled a small notebook out of his back pocket and was carefully plotting his attack on the course. Jones was looking through his bag, counting clubs. I wondered, just for an instant, if I could be imagining this whole scene.

Hell, I thought, I don't care if I am. I'm playing with these guys today.

Jones looked up at me and smiled, as if aware of my uncertainty. He put a warm hand on my arm, and it felt as real as anything. He slid his famous putter, Calamity Jane, out of his bag and said, "Let's practice our putting before the others arrive."

We ambled toward the practice green, leaving Hogan to his privacy. He seemed to prefer it that way.

When we were out of earshot, Jones began talking again. "I've always known someone would come to us. When you're ready, Zachary, you must record what happens here today."

"But—" I began.

Jones held up a hand to silence me. "There's a spiritual order to golf, a flow that—once understood—can be mastered." Jones hesitated, as if wondering whether to say more; then he changed the subject deftly. "This course has been here for centuries."

I followed his lead and looked at the course that lay before us. For the most part, it was an open, natural course. A driving range was off to the side of the mountain, and a practice putting green was tucked near the clubhouse.

"Unlike Scottish courses, where the accepted principle is nine holes out to a distant point and back," Jones said, "this course is a prototype of modern golf course architecture. The swirling loops challenge the golfer with wind. No more than three successive holes pursue the same direction, forcing you to play the winds from all sides."

As in life? I wondered to myself. Where people sometimes struggle against the wind in their faces and at other times are helped by the wind at their backs?

"Who designed this course?" I asked.

"West Wind evolved. It's been here always, God's playing field for humans. Look at the bunkers." Jones pointed to the bear-claw bunker I'd noticed on the first hole. "That bunker is a natural depression, created from centuries of sheltering animals. That one in particular used to shelter mountain sheep, if I'm not mistaken."

I looked at Jones, meeting his glittering eyes, and then back at the course again. I saw what he saw: heavy rough carpeted with mountain wildflowers rather than grass, deep sandy bunkers crafted by the hand of time, a sparkling brook created from melting mountain snow. I was puzzled, though, by the apparently Native American markings on the course. A bunker in the shape of a bear claw? And I saw other bunkers that looked like arrowheads.

Jones reached into his pocket and pulled out three balls, dropping them onto the putting green—an elevated, figure-eight green with a dozen pins, and slopes of every conceivable angle.

I stood in awe as Jones gripped Calamity Jane and began practicing. His first putt lay about five feet from the cup. He stood slightly open, his left foot back from the line, heels close together.

His touch was perfect. Calamity Jane, barely stroking her target, sent the ball flowing toward the hole. Clunk.

He moved his second ball out another five feet, increasing the distance between himself and the cup. He took a longer backswing this time, longer than I'd ever taken. The clubhead slowly gained momentum, but the impact was so gentle that I hardly heard the club rap the ball.

The ball aimed dead center, as if a chalk line had been drawn in the grass from Jones's clubhead to the center of the hole. Clunk. It dropped in.

Jones pulled his third ball back another ten feet away for a twenty-foot putt. His backswing was even more graceful this time; Calamity Jane sang a simple, soothing lullaby. And his timing was perfect. Clunk. His third putt dropped.

All of sudden, I realized that this man before me—Bobby Jones—had been dead for five years. It was 1976, and he had died in 1971. The flag at my home golf course had been flown at half mast on the day Jones died. I remembered seeing pictures of his funeral. Walter Cronkite's gravelly voice on the evening news had declared, "The world of golf will never be the same. Today, Bobby Jones is dead."

And yet before me—impossibly—stood Bobby Jones.

He had the same beautifully languid rhythm I'd seen in his instructional films. He carried himself with the same grace and poise I'd seen in his pictures. And Calamity Jane was the same worn and scarred putter I'd seen in the Golf House museum.

"Are you really dead?" I whispered.

Jones's legendary blue eyes softened.

"I . . . I mean, I saw pictures of your funeral," I stammered.

He silently weighed his words before responding. "All of the great religions," he began, "believe in a life after this one. Christianity. Judaism. Buddhism. They all teach that death isn't the end, but the journey back to the One.

"It's easy for us to believe that Jesus lived and died, and that he lives still. Many of us feel Jesus' presence at difficult times in our lives. I myself have felt his presence.

"Still, it's difficult for us to comprehend the nature of death as it applies to *us*."

Jones slowly bent down to pick up his golf balls. One, two, and then three. He slid them back into his pocket.

"There are many layers to reality," he said. "All of the universe is energy. Your body is energy, although in a very dense form. It's easy for you to understand that your body is in a constant cycle of re-birth. Individual cells are always dying and being reborn. In fact, every few years, every single cell in your body is replaced.

"But the soul? That's more difficult to comprehend. The soul is energy also, but a lighter, more transient force. It's possible to re-turn, though, to stay in such a deep connection with material en-ergy that your spirit is drawn back. So it is with me and golf. Although I'm dead, although my body has passed on, my spirit is connected forever to the game that I love. And I'm here."

Jones's spirit filled me with awe. I knew what he was talking about; he was describing what I felt every time I played golf.

Jones offered a shy grin and handed me his putter. I reached out and took Calamity Jane. She looked like an ordinary putter, but she felt like magic. Her grip was soft leather, her iron head battle-scarred. This was the putter that had won the Impregnable Quadrilateral: the U.S. Amateur, the U.S. Open, the British Amateur, and the British Open.

My hands started to shake.

Jones laughed. "She's just a putter. A *fabulous* putter, but still just a putter."

Well, I thought, Jones might be dead, but Calamity Jane was very much alive.

Jones dropped his three balls onto the green for me to hit. He nodded his approval as I gripped Calamity Jane.

I sank my five-foot putt, my ten-footer sped right toward the hole—and right past it—and my twenty-foot putt dropped cleanly. I was pleased. For my first experience with Calamity Jane, putting in front of Bobby Jones, I hadn't made too big a fool out of myself.

"You'll play with Walter first," Jones said, interrupting my reverie.

"Walter *Hagen?*"

"Yes. There's an order to these things, you know. You'll play with Walter first."

THE HAIG WAS LATE.

The other players had arrived while Jones and I were talking on the putting green. I stood quietly on the first tee, in awe of the crowd around me.

It looked as if a picture book on golf had suddenly come to life. A young Arnold Palmer stood shoulder-to-shoulder with Jack Nicklaus. Ben Hogan stood practicing his swing. Bobby Jones was fielding questions from Byron Nelson and Tony Lema. Gary Player, South Africa's man in black, was politely quiet but obviously anxious to get started. With the exception of Player and Hogan, everyone seemed to be complaining.

"Why do you always put him first?"

"You know he's always late!"

"*I'm* not in charge of the tee times. *Who put Hagen first?*"

Hogan, who stood apart, absorbed in his own world, looked over and caught me in his steely gaze. He made me very uncomfortable. Unlike Jones, who'd looked at me with soft acceptance, Hogan looked at me with a knowledge of stark reality. I felt trapped, cornered, as if he alone knew my frailties. Perhaps this was why the sportswriters of the late forties had called Hogan "the Ice Man." If any one of these masters could break my concentration, it was Hogan.

I DIDN'T DESERVE TO BE in the company of such great golfers. Hogan's unwavering gaze reminded me of that. After all, I still struggled with my swing. My putting was far from perfect. I was no champion.

Then again, I'd been a promising golfer once, and not so long ago. I'd won two caddie championships. I'd even caddied for Billy Hyndman III, one of the top-ten amateurs in the country back in the late fifties. Billy had told me that I was a great caddie, that he couldn't have won without me.

Yes, I knew what to do on the golf course. I had an uncanny eye for distances. I knew which clubs to use. I even followed Hogan's written edict to always overclub in case of wind.

But somehow it all got messed up in the translation from my head to my body. Golf, for me, was a physical manifestation of my inner hang-ups. When I doubted myself, which—if I have to admit the truth—was often, I hooked the ball. Then I got mad. The perfection, the beautiful harmony of golf, seemed to elude me.

I could feel it in my heart; I just couldn't always *do* it.

I think that's why I started looking to the champions. When one person achieves greatness, it shows us what's possible. It's almost as if our own internal circuitry were wired for greatness, if only we could figure out how to align ourselves with this stronger current.

Ben Hogan had figured it out. So had Bobby Jones. So had every other man on this course today.

When I wasn't on a golf course, I read everything I could about the golfing greats. When I finished reading all the famous sportswriting on golf—columns and books by Herbert Warren Wind, Charles Price, and Grantland Rice—I turned to biographies. I found I liked them better than news reports, because they helped me understand my heroes. When I read *The Walter Hagen Story,* I met the great Haig. When I read *Golf Is My Game,* I saw Bobby Jones, the southern gentleman. I fell in love with golf's personalities.

THE HAIG HAD ARRIVED.

He took huge, pounding steps toward us, the golf course trembling at his appearance. Confidence oozed from him. "So, have you all decided who's going to place second today?" Hagen asked, laughing as he joined the assembled crowd.

Jones stepped forward, obviously the leader. He shook Hagen's hand warmly and clasped him on the shoulder. "Walter, may I introduce you to Zachary?" Jones motioned me forward. "He'll be playing with you today. At least for the first few holes."

Hagen looked me up and down. "Well, son, you're not the smartest dresser, but you'll have to do. I'll see what I can do about improving your taste."

Everyone laughed.

I looked down at my outfit. I was wearing simple khaki pants, white golf shoes, and a collared sports shirt.

Hagen, however, showed how a real golfer should dress. His attire was perfectly coordinated for the gentleman's game. He wore white flannel trousers that looked as pristine as a coating of new snow. His black sleeveless pullover harmonized with a white silk shirt, a dark tie, and black-and-white golf shoes.

I was thoroughly intimidated.

The other golfers began to disperse. Nicklaus followed Hogan to the driving range. Player, Palmer, and Lema laughed together as they headed toward the practice putting green.

Only Byron Nelson remained with us, standing tall and lanky on the first tee. He was obviously Hagen's playing partner.

"Walter, you'll play with Byron as usual," Jones said. Then he turned to me. "Play with Walter. When you're ready for your next lesson, you'll know what to do."

And with the soft brush of his words, Jones left the three of us alone.

THE FIRST HOLE SUDDENLY seemed to change in appearance. The course took on an old-timey patina. The rough became rougher, the greens hard and unwatered. In that single moment, when Jones stepped off the tee, I was catapulted back into the glory days of golf: the twenties and thirties. The days of Walter Hagen and a young Byron Nelson.

I took a good look at the Haig.

His black hair gleamed like oiled sealskin above a tanned, weather-beaten face. His smile was broad, his tie perfectly knotted beneath his cashmere vest. His pants were the woolliest, his vest the fleeciest, his shirt the silkiest.

Hagen was a solid man, not particularly tall but a little over-weight. He held himself, though, with absolute poise, as if his extra pounds were a sign of affluence, the desirable result of filet mignon dinners and champagne cocktails.

He unsheathed his driver with panache and tipped the brim of an imaginary cap, gesturing, I supposed, to imaginary fans. His movements were expansive, generous. His grandiosity wasn't in the way he moved; rather, it was in the feelings he exuded.

I looked down the fairway. It was the same undulating carpet I'd seen before, but somehow the green patina now bowed in Hagen's honor, not mine. Byron Nelson stood off to the side practicing his swing. He seemed to be as much in awe of Hagen as I was.

Hagen motioned to me, and I recognized that he was giving me honors.

I'd have felt much better caddying for Hagen than playing in front of him. I was so nervous I wasn't sure if I could play anything that even *resembled* golf.

Hagen motioned again, obviously enjoying my discomfort.

I teed my ball and decided to try to drive it exactly as I had before. I picked out a spot on the fairway to aim at, waggled, and swung.

The sun glinted across the white of my ball as it began to rise. I smiled involuntarily as a rush of wind swelled in my heart, moving in tandem with my ball.

Then the ball began to curve ever so slightly to the right.

I motioned left, hoping to push it back to the center of the fairway with the sheer weight of my intention. The ball kept on curving toward the trees as if drawn by a magnet.

Hagen laughed.

Nelson's face flushed, and I knew he was embarrassed for me.

We heard the treetops rustle. My ball had been trapped by the cluster of pines.

"It'll play." Hagen laughed again.

He teed up his own ball. He barely took time to select a target; he simply waggled and swung, lunging forward as he did so. As he moved all of his weight into the ball, his odd stance reminded me of a baseball player's posture.

The Haig calmly watched his ball fly low and then rise to follow the same curving path my ball had flown, straight into the trees.

Hagen smiled, obviously pleased with his shot.

I looked at him in disbelief. "Did you *mean* to do that?"

"Chaos is the first step," he declared.

"No single golf shot is the final result. If you call it a bad shot, then you don't really understand what's going on. Sometimes a bad shot puts you in a *better* position than a so-called good one," Hagen said.

"After all, I expect a certain number of wild shots per round. So when I hit a wild one, I know it's all part of the plan. I don't let it bother me. An *avalanche* of mistakes couldn't bother me."

With that, the Haig swaggered through the trees, looking for all the world like someone accustomed to swaggering through palaces.

We found our balls nestled in the midst of three tall pine trees; Hagen's was right next to mine. Nelson had fired his ball right down the center of the fairway.

I surveyed the path out. One tree was about ten yards directly in front of my ball. I couldn't hit forward; I'd have to chip out and continue from there.

After I'd chipped my ball safely onto the fairway, Hagen strode up to his ball, ready to take his second swing. He looked straight toward the pin as if the interfering pine tree were nonexistent, pulled back, and hit his ball. It flew right past the tree, clearing it by only inches, then bumped and ran toward the green, just barely missing the guarding bunker.

It was an absolutely perfect second shot. Hagen was now in position for a birdie.

My mouth hung open. He had made the difficult—no, the impossible—look perfectly *natural*.

"How . . . ?" I questioned.

Hagen smiled once again, and his teeth, as perfectly white as his flannel trousers, gleamed brightly. "You have to become comfortable with the chaos. I make more bad shots in a single season than anyone else. Lucky for me, I realized long ago that I'm just human. I'm going to make plenty of shots that make me look like the rankest amateur—like hitting a ball into the woods."

My face reddened at the comparison.

Hagen continued: "But if I'd let a blunder like that get to me, I'd have kicked away every championship or challenge match I've ever played.

"I've learned not to call something *bad* until I know the whole story. Some of my wildest shots have led me to my greatest victories. Chaos can be good."

I STARTED SEARCHING FOR THE CHAOS in my own life. Was it possible that something bad could turn out to be good, as Hagen claimed?

I remembered a woman I'd dated when I was in my early twenties, before I got married. She was a beautiful blond, tall and willowy, and I was desperately in love with her. I'd have done anything for her.

She was elusive, and I was always pursuing her. She broke dates with me and sneaked around with other men, but when I caught her, she professed to love me passionately. We'd have two or maybe three months of happiness before she'd go back to her old games. It was as if she were driving me away on purpose. Well, after a few years, I finally took the hint.

Then, much to my surprise, I met a tiny brunette whom I later married. She was nothing like my first girlfriend—and by then, I was glad of it. She was petite and truthful to the core. If I'd met her a few years earlier, I wouldn't have looked twice.

Was this what Hagen was talking about? That chaos was actually part of the plan? That it helped you develop a new way of looking at life? That what seemed bad could ultimately turn out to be good?

I thought about my job. I'd recently been promoted, but instead of being happy, I felt as though I'd been shot into the woods, just like my golf ball.

I had a new boss, one who blamed me for problems that weren't under my control. I'd tried the safe route—reasoning with him—but it had made no difference. Was this a little like chipping out onto the fairway? Taking the safe and accepted route but setting yourself up for a bogey anyway?

Perhaps, like Hagen, I could develop new skills to deal with the chaos. After all, chaos wasn't the supreme ruler, just a step in the process. Perhaps I could learn to be a better leader—to correct the problems even if they weren't my fault. Perhaps this would lead me to a *bigger* promotion later. Perhaps it was all part of the plan.

WE PLAYED OUT THE HOLE. I hit a nice mid-iron to the green and two-putted for a bogey. Nelson continued his steady performance with fairways and greens, one-putting for a birdie. Hagen two-putted for par.

As we walked to the second hole, a par five, I caught sight of a small, old-fashioned leaderboard. It read:

Nelson	-1
Hagen	even par
Tobias	+1

It was thrilling to see! Anyone who's ever imagined joining the pro tour has visualized the day when his name is alongside those of the greats. And here was mine. I might be third, but I was up there! I started wondering if it was possible, even *remotely* possible, that I might win.

"Let me tell you a story," Hagen said as we drove off the tee.

I was all ears.

"It was the 1914 U.S. Open. It was only the second Open I'd ever played in, and I was determined to win.

"Well, I like to live well, and that tournament was no exception." He laughed. "The night before the first round, I went out for a lobster dinner. My wallet couldn't manage the style I wanted to become accustomed to, and so the restaurant wasn't quite the best.

"That night, I woke up at about three in the morning with horrible stomach cramps. The lobster hadn't been fresh, and I had food poisoning. I didn't think I'd be able to play—I could hardly walk—but I just couldn't go back home to Rochester and say that my own foolishness had kept me from playing. So I played.

"That day, I was wilder than ever before or since. I was all over the course. I think I hit every single drive into the rough.

"Then the magic of chaos happened. My mind was so occupied with the pain in my stomach that I didn't even think about each shot I made. I didn't worry at all. I just did what I needed to do.

"Putting was always my strength, and that day, at one point, I needed only seven putts on nine consecutive holes. I wanted to get back to my hotel room to rest!

"Now, I wouldn't recommend a case of food poisoning as a way of forgetting to worry about a golf score, but it taught me to look at each round as a unit and to take individual bad shots in stride.

"Anyone else would have said that getting food poisoning on the eve of the U.S. Open was a bad thing. But it wasn't. It was the chaos that led me to my first major victory."

I looked up and saw that we'd just holed out. Like Hagen, I'd forgotten to worry. Chaos was working in my favor.

I'd hit a marvelous twenty-foot putt for birdie—putting me at even par. Hagen, ever lackadaisical, had taken his full five shots to stay at even par. Nelson had crafted another workman-like birdie. He was in the lead at two under.

But I was up there, too.

ALL OF A SUDDEN, Hagen got serious.

He looked at the leaderboard and saw that Nelson had crept ahead with a quiet, studious game. Hagen straightened himself up; the big-game hunter was stalking his prey.

The tournament was on.

I was reminded of a book I'd read in college: *The Magic Mountain* by Thomas Mann. "There are two ways to life," Mann had written. "One is the regular, direct, and good way; the other is bad, it leads through death, and this is the way of the genius." The way most people see life is the way of mediocrity—not too much pain, but not too much pleasure either. The way of the genius is to know that pain creates beauty. That destruction creates magnificence.

This was Hagen's way.

He strutted to the tee. It was a long par three, 194 yards. The tee shot was over water. The green was large but well trapped to the left and rear. If you were short, you'd splash your ball, but if you were long, you'd have a very difficult sand shot to the green.

I knew logically that the problems of this hole were predominantly psychological, but frankly, this course was beginning to intimidate me.

I winced as Hagen selected a four-iron. The wind was against him, and I thought he needed more club. But as Hagen lunged at the ball, I could have sworn the wind picked up in force to help him. The Haig's ball lofted gracefully, landing five feet from the pin. Hagen was in line for his birdie.

Nelson chose a three-iron, as I did, and both of our shots landed a comfortable distance from the pin, safely on the green— away from the water and away from the traps. We both two-putted.

Nelson had protected his lead, I stayed at even par, and Hagen moved forward to one under. The chaos was working in his favor.

"HAVE YOU EVER BEEN TO HAWAII, Zachary?" Hagen asked unexpectedly as we stood on the edge of the green.

"Yes, actually. I took my wife there on our honeymoon." I was beginning to enjoy Hagen's teaching method. His conversation was as wild and unpredictable as his drives.

"I was in Hawaii in the mid-forties with Joe Kirkwood. We did a world tour together—he did the trick shots, and I played exhibition matches. It was quite a lot of fun." Hagen smiled at the memory.

"Hawaii?" I reminded him.

"Oh, yes. Hawaii. Do you know why the Hawaiian Islands are so lush?"

"Why?"

"After the volcanoes erupted—hundreds of years after—the ash created a new soil, richer than before. The once-hot lava flourished into a paradise with palm trees and hibiscus plants."

I looked at Hagen and knew he wasn't talking about golf. He meant that there was an extraordinary order in the pattern of chaos. The cosmos was filled with seemingly random and destructive events, but in the end, things fell apart simply to come together again in a more magnificent way.

Hagen was staring at me, dark eyes glittering with pleasure. He knew I understood.

He picked up his ball and thrust it into his pocket. As we looked toward the next hole, I saw a million blades of grass waving in the wind, shafts of sunlight with dancing specks of dust captured within, and the footprints of a thousand golfers who'd fallen in and out of love with this course.

There was a glorious pattern to our existence, though each blade of grass was random and chaotic, seemingly without pattern. When viewed together, it was a carpet of life.

"There's a perfect plan at every point in your life," he said, "even when it looks as if things have gone awry. Golf is the same way. You're playing the perfect game at all times, even if you don't realize it. Golf gives you what you need most—which sometimes is an opportunity to improve on certain shots.

"When you stop resisting the plan that's unfolding—when you submit to it—you can see that there *is* a plan behind the chaos. It's then that your own greatness can emerge."

He paused for a moment and then turned back to me.

"Step back from your golf, Zachary," he instructed. "See the beauty in each shot you hit. No matter where it lands, know there's a perfect round of golf that's trying to emerge. No matter how chaotic the outcome, everything is leading you toward this perfect plan. You must trust."

With that, the Haig laughed, and I saw him draw his mask of confidence around himself once more. He smoothed his trousers and then bent down to wipe an imaginary spot off his gleaming shoes.

I SAT ON A SMALL BENCH, alone, at the tee box of the fourth hole. Hagen and Nelson had gone on without me. They'd told me to wait for the next pairing.

Nelson had assured me, though, with uncomplicated enthusiasm, that we would get a chance to talk, he and I, before the day was over.

The leaderboard still had Nelson at two under. I wondered how it was updated. Was Nelson still leading as he played through, or had Hagen stalked into first place?

Trust. Hagen's last word echoed in my ears. I remembered my honeymoon in Hawaii. My wife and I had taken one of those plantation tours and seen a Hawaiian man doing a rain dance.

"Does the rain dance really bring rain?" we'd asked with a laugh.

"Oh, yes," he replied. "The rain dance *always* brings rain. Sometimes it works in a few minutes, sometimes a few days. Other times it takes a year or two, but the rain dance always brings rain. Sometimes it brings floods."

He was right. The rains always came eventually, didn't they? We Westerners are trained to believe in only what we can see. Growing beyond chaos requires trust in what we *can't* see—indeed, trust in a process that at first glance looks bad.

The challenge of golf is trust also. You train your swing and hone it through practice, and then you must trust it completely. You can't *think* about swinging; you must simply trust.

I was capable of making magic shots when I was in high school. Back then, I'd been a wizard around the green. If I hit a wild iron to the green, I simply saved it with a twenty-five-foot birdie putt. I couldn't hole putts like that anymore. I didn't trust myself.

If a Hawaiian can trust that lava will create paradise, that a rain dance will bring rain, perhaps I could learn to trust myself. To trust in the absolute goodness of life, even when confronted by chaos.

Yes, I thought, I could.

Suddenly, I felt good, better than I had in years. Jones was right: golf *was* the path to spiritual learning, and finally I was on it.

3   *The Secret of Unity*

Hagen reawakened a dream in me, one I'd long since buried.

I started playing golf when I was thirteen years old. Within six months, I'd broken 80, and within twelve months, I was regularly playing at par. It was all so easy that I never realized how rare my gift was. That's why I let my parents talk me out of taking that golf scholarship. All I'd known was the magic. How was I to know that scholarships and perfect golf were such rare and precious things?

After that, life got harder.

I dropped out of college and didn't dare think about golf. I did what everyone expected of me: I got a job, got married, and had a kid. Buying a house, providing a secure future for my family—these were the important things in my life. I missed my daughter's first steps and first words and first dance recital, but that was the way things had to be. I was on the road earning a good living.

The more compromises I made in my life, the more my game fell apart, until finally, at the age of twenty-three, I quit playing altogether.

Things fall apart to come together again in a new way, Hagen had said. What was making my life fall apart? My compromises. They hadn't made me happy; they'd robbed me of my dreams. And what is a man without dreams? He's someone who wants a chance to be special—to really *be* someone—but who's afraid the golf scholarship of his youth was his only opportunity.

As I was thinking these sober thoughts, I recognized the man who possessed enough glue to make life come together again. He came over the small rise that separated the third and fourth holes, looking like a sage cloaked in black. He wore a black sports shirt, black sweater, slim black pants, and black shoes. Even his golf glove was black. It was Gary Player, and I knew at once that of all the golfers on the course today, Player was the one who could help me recapture my lost dream.

Player himself had overcome tremendous odds to become a champion, battling not only the game itself but his own lack of size and strength. Player was only five feet seven inches tall. On top of that, he'd been a skinny, underdeveloped kid.

But his was an indomitable spirit. Player had channeled his tremendous creative and emotional energies into his game and had made the most of his physical attributes. He'd done what only three other golfers in history had accomplished—he'd won all four majors: the Masters, the U.S. Open, the PGA Championship, and the British Open.

"Hello, Zachary," he said softly, and my heart swelled at his call.

Player sounded as I'd always imagined he would. His voice was a mélange of soft colonial tones and gentle British rhythms mixed with a faint memory of Dutch. Hearing his voice, I felt a primal stirring in my heart. He sounded like Africa.

With a voodoo prescience, he asked the question that burned within me. "Tell me, Zachary," he asked, "what are your dreams?"

Looking into Player's gentle eyes, I felt a wave of total acceptance. Gary Player would help me; I knew he would.

"I want to play one round of perfect golf," I said softly.

And then I told him everything about myself. My regrets. The lost magic. The nagging feeling that I'd given it all up when I was too young and naive to know better.

"Sometimes I'll hit an incredible drive," I said, "or sink a really long putt. There'll be just enough magic to let me know it's lurking. Then, after a few great holes, I fall apart again. I can't do it for a whole round."

Player looked out at the course, lost in thought. The dew was still fresh on the fairway, and it sparkled like a sea of diamonds.

When he turned back to me, his voice was soft. "Do you believe in God?"

"*God?*" I asked. "What does God have to do with shooting a perfect score?"

Player laughed, his brown eyes crinkling. "You're a being of spirit, Zachary. There's a part of you that was alive long before you were born, a part of you that will live on long after death."

Player reminded me of Jones. He'd talked about spirituality, too, about a presence different and apart from religion. About a dimension of faith that comes to you from beyond the walls of a church. When I was on a golf course, I felt this presence. It came to me each time I played, as I sensed the eternal steps of everyone who'd ever loved the game walking in tandem with me. That's what made Player's words all the more frustrating. I knew what he was talking about. I could feel the magic. I just couldn't do it.

"Think of Seve Ballesteros," Player said. "He was once one of the world's greatest players. Like Walter Hagen, he was never bothered by a wild drive. He played magic shots from bunkers, from trees, even from parking lots. Then, somewhere along the way, he lost his innocence. He stopped believing in the magic."

"Like me," I replied. The memories of magic putts and wizard-like chip shots—shots I couldn't make today—flooded my mind.

"You must lose your innocence in order to find it again," Player said gently. "There's another, greater evolutionary leap going on within all of us—within Ballesteros and within you, too, Zachary."

My wife had called my struggles with golf an early midlife crisis. I had a feeling Player would agree.

"You must find out who you truly are, Zachary," Player said. "Not who society has made you, but who you truly are."

HE TOLD ME about his own journey.

"At the 1972 PGA Championship, I was one up after the third round, but I didn't feel secure. There were four other golfers pushing right behind me. Everyone was hungry to win.

"Worse, I felt very out of balance. The tournament was held at Oakland Hills in Detroit—dubbed 'the Monster' by Ben Hogan in 1951. It's a long course and an incredibly punishing one. I had to struggle with my drives to keep up with everyone else.

"On Sunday morning before teeing off, I called home to South Africa to speak with my father. He said, 'Don't worry about what everyone else is doing. Just go out there and win it for me, Gary.' I knew what I had to do. I had to play the way I, Gary Player, was capable of playing. Not the way every other golfer played, not trying to outdrive everyone, and not doing what the fans or sportscasters expected of me.

"I confounded everyone with my shot on the sixteenth hole. From the wet rough, with the pin completely hidden by a willow tree, and with a lake standing between me and the hole, I shot directly at the green. My nine-iron lofted over both the tree and the lake and gave me a three-foot birdie putt. I won the tournament by two strokes. It wasn't the daring shot that won it for me, though. It was the fact that I let my spirit take the lead and my body was in the right condition to follow its commands.

"You see, Zachary, if your mind and body aren't in perfect alignment, you get very uneven and unpredictable results. During the first three days of that tournament, I played everyone else's game— and ignored my own spirit. On Sunday, my father's simple words reminded me of what it takes to be a champion: when your body and spirit are in perfect unity, all the disjointed elements of your game simply fall away.

"Would you like to learn how to find unity?" he asked.

I nodded greedily.

I WAS FALLING THROUGH SPACE.

Player's words echoed in my head: *All the disjointed elements simply fall away.* The gently rolling mountainscape of West Wind, with its red earth and cultivated evergreens, undulated and then changed before my eyes. One minute I was in Utah; the next minute I was on what appeared to be a dusty mine trail in the hills of . . . *South Africa?*

Player was a few feet ahead of me.

"Where are we?" I asked, my voice full of wonder.

"Johannesburg," he replied, laughing. "We're going for a run."

I looked down and saw two pairs of running shoes at our feet. One of them was a size twelve. My size. Player pulled on his shoes and started running. I had no choice but to follow him. The road, caked with dry red earth, threaded upward through the hills.

After only a half-mile, my legs were aching.

"What . . . are . . . we . . . doing?" I huffed.

"Synchronizing body and spirit," he said. He wasn't a bit winded. His voice carried the same rhythmic tones as always.

"I've been meaning to exercise more, but there never seems to be enough time . . ." My voice trailed off.

"If you knew how important exercise is to your spiritual life, you'd be drawn to it just as I am." Player picked up the pace, and I had to struggle to keep up. "When I was a young teenager, I knew that if I ever wanted to become a champion golfer, I had to work harder than anyone else. So to build up my legs, I ran. My brother Ian always went with me, up and down these dusty gold-mine hills. When I wanted to quit after running only a mile or so, he wouldn't let me. Because of Ian, I came to realize that I could keep going even when I thought I couldn't.

"Later, when I played in a tournament and wanted to quit, when I was tired or scared or racked by nerves, I remembered these hills. I remembered that you *can* keep going. You can always try just a little bit harder."

My legs ached. I was more out of shape than I wanted to admit, but Player made sense. I could keep going just a little bit longer. I wasn't a quitter. Far from it. My co-workers, my wife, even my daughter—they all admired my determination. I dug down a little deeper, and I could swear my legs felt a little less tired. I kept pace with Player.

"This is how I synchronize my body and spirit," he explained. "A run through the hills of Johannesburg. No matter where I am, I can return in my mind to these dusty mine trails and thereby bring the power of my home with me.

"You can do many things to bring unity into your life, Zachary. Exercise is just one of the most effective. During exercise, you become intimately aware of the beingness of your body. You feel each muscle as it stretches; you become aware of every part of your physical self.

"This process—this routine of unity—is like a meditation," he explained. "It allows you to step into a bubble, into a quiet world separate from everyone else, a world where nothing can distract you. If you concentrate on aligning your body and spirit before you do anything important—before a golf match, before an important sales presentation," he smiled at me, "even before going to bed at night—you can make your body a vessel for the Divine.

"If you put everything you have into everything you do, you won't have regrets. You won't have a past you want to re-do."

As our steps pounded out the rhythm of unity, I thought about what Player had said. I was a being of spirit but also a body of flesh. It made sense that I had to unite the two. Was this how Player had found the courage to be himself? How I might find it, too?

We reached the peak of the mountain, and I saw Johannesburg spread before me. It was a city of contrasts. Ultramodern corporate towers and bustling city traffic lay at its heart, but farther out, on the edges of town, were shabby shantytowns, hard and rural. Farther still were the beautiful hills of South Africa, green and rolling.

"Johannesburg is the City of Gold," Player explained. "South Africa is the world's largest gold producer. The 300-mile 'golden arc' stretches from the Eastern Transvaal through Johannesburg along the Wes Wits line to the freestate gold fields.

"Johannesburg in 1976 is a land of separateness and contrast. It's ironic, I suppose, that the city sits atop the world's richest vein of gold, atop so much promise. It's also here in Soweto, the Johannesburg South Western Township, that the blight of apartheid is showcased in all its grotesque ugliness.

"It's the same with people. Our spirits are a gold mine, but we remain in a land of poverty because we don't synchronize the two."

The iron tenderness of South Africa wove a spell around us. When Player finally spoke again, his voice was tinged with sadness. "I've had my own struggles, Zachary, with what society has tried to make me.

"As the world highlighted South Africa's problem of apartheid, I've been made accountable." Player's feet sounded a gentle, steady rhythm, symbolic of his determined presence. "There have been death threats against me. When I played in the '72 PGA Championship, while I struggled with unity, I had to have police protection. Demonstrators have thrown rotten fruit at me. Once," he laughed sardonically, "even a cup of ice. I was called a racist simply because of the color of my skin.

"Many of my friends suggested that I could avoid the problems—the demonstrators and the death threats—by simply moving to the United States. It would have been easier to follow society's rules, to publicly shun the apartheid government. But that's not who I am.

"When I look at South Africa, Zachary, I see a country where all races on earth are represented. Blacks. Indians. Whites. Coloreds. There are a hundred different shades of skin color." Player's voice took on a reverential tone. "Did you know that South Africa has more racial groups within her borders than almost any other country on earth? Our people speak many languages: English, Xhosa, Zulu, Afrikaans—the list is endless.

"I see within South Africa a chance for unity. A chance for our people to live together in harmony, strengthened—not diminished—by our diversity. I've stayed because *this* was the path of my spirit, to change from within. The harder path, but *my* path."

As Player spoke, I understood—for the first time, I think—how golf is a microcosm of life. We must all learn to play our own game. Just as Player had done on the golf course, every person must find the path of his or her spirit.

A GENTLE WESTERLY WIND STARTED BLOWING, time shifted, and we were back at West Wind.

The rocky desert mountains of Utah looked so different from the hills of Johannesburg, and yet I felt a certain connection between the two. As if all people, and all landscapes, were part of a greater whole.

"How do you feel now?" Player asked.

"Actually," I said with a laugh, "I feel calmer. Does this make any sense? I was anxious before we started running. For the first mile, my muscles were tense. But then all my worries started to fade away."

"That's exactly why I exercise," Player said. "I'm not just a health nut, although some have called me that. There's a practical, positive reason for everything I do. Exercise doesn't just make you fit; it synchronizes body and spirit. If I'm feeling down or fearful, the first thing I do is head for my weight-training equipment. I've learned that if I can just get started—just give my body ten or fifteen minutes of exercise—it will clear my mind and refocus my spirit."

I nodded with understanding. Exercise was a practical application of unity. It wasn't only for the body; it was also for the soul.

"You'll enjoy this story," Player continued. "Every year before the Masters Championship in Augusta, the past winners get together for dinner. The reigning champion pays for it.

"Well, one year, we had more fun than normal and stayed up talking past eleven o'clock in the evening. I knew I should go to bed as soon as we parted company, but this was Masters week. I stayed up until after midnight doing my exercises. I needed the unity they'd bring me.

"I stayed up late on Saturday night, too, doing my exercises again before the final round. And they gave me the extra push I needed: on Sunday I went out and shot a 64, equaled the course record, and won another green jacket."

"When was this?" I asked. I couldn't remember Player ever shooting a 64 in the final round of the Masters.

He smiled cryptically. "Two years from now."

THE FOURTH HOLE BECKONED TO US. The sand traps called to Player and his magnificent bunker skill, and the swooping fairway sang a song of harmony to me. Player's innocence and single-mindedness had begun to rub off. I felt the lure of a birdie. I pulled out my driver and took two complete practice swings.

The hole was a par four, 428 yards long. The fairway swooped downhill and swung sharply to the right. A cluster of bunkers in the shape of a bear claw guarded the inner edge of the dogleg. My stomach growled, and for that single moment, I wondered if a driver was my best choice. If I tried to cut over the dogleg to set myself up for a birdie, there was a good chance of catching the bunker. But if I took the long route around the far edge, I'd almost certainly make par. I looked to see which club Player had chosen. He held his driver, so I held onto mine, too. I wanted that birdie.

Player hit first.

He wound up his body and unfurled his entire spirit into his drive. He carried the dogleg and cleared the nest of bunkers cleanly. My drive, while infinitely less confident, also cleared the right turn. I barely missed the bunkers and landed in the rough of mountain wildflowers. Not too bad, though.

Our second shots were uphill, and the wind, at my back on the third hole, was now coming at me. I pulled a three-iron from my bag. Player chose a two-iron. Hesitating for a moment, I wondered if I should follow Player's lead.

Deferring to his expertise, I quietly slipped my three-iron back into my bag and pulled out a two-iron.

Player hit his shot cleanly to the center of the green while mine went long, hit the top of the green, and bounced off the upper edge. I was left with a directly downhill lie, and the greens were hard, fast, and unwatered. I'd need a small miracle to sink my putt.

Damn. I chastised myself for my poor club selection. If I hadn't second-guessed myself, I could have birdied this hole and hung onto even par for the round. As it stood now, I'd almost certainly bogey and drop back even farther in competition.

As if on cue, my stomach rumbled again.

"WHAT DID YOU EAT FOR BREAKFAST?" Player asked, laughing. "That growling is going to interrupt my putting." We walked toward the green through a spray of dew.

"I was pretty busy this morning, rushing to get to the course and all," I mumbled.

"Nothing?" Player was surprised.

I hung my head in mock shame.

"And you wonder why you chose the wrong club!" he exclaimed. "Anytime your game falls apart, you have to stop and re-synchronize body and spirit. Unity isn't something you do once—like taking a run. It's a way of living."

Player rummaged in his golf bag and then handed me a small plastic bag. It was full of raisins, nuts, dried fruit, and . . .

"African mealie-mealie. It's a kind of grain," he explained. "This is my personal snack mix. I never go on the course without it. After all," he added with a chuckle, "who knows when I'll need a quick body-spirit alignment?"

I gingerly pulled a few pieces of fruit from the bag, and—to my delight—they were delicious. I greedily ate a few more handfuls. The mix was crunchy and tasty and nourishing. I felt a magical pulse surge throughout my body.

Player smiled broadly. I think he took as much pleasure in my learning as I did.

He motioned for me to putt.

The green shimmered around us like an emerald city. I was only twenty feet away from the cup, but it was a precipitous slide into eternity. I rapped the ball a little too quickly, and it flew past the hole. I looked at Player questioningly, but he shook his head and said, "You have to play your own game, Zachary. Find your own path to the hole."

Player stroked his ball in for a birdie, and it was my turn again.

I laid my putter down and squatted next to it. I was ten feet away, but this time I was under the pin. A much easier place to be. I considered the straight line to the hole, but then—amazingly—I noticed a slight undulation right before the cup. If I aimed straight, my ball would break right.

I took two gentle practice swings, stepped up to the ball, and aimed just a hair left of the cup. The ball rolled directly along my mental line, and just before the cup, it broke right. Clunk. I'd saved par.

THE FIFTH HOLE at West Wind gave me a chance to test out all my new theories. It didn't require exceptional athletic skill; instead, it demanded exceptional coordination between mind and body.

The hole was a long par three, only 195 yards. I wondered about the men who had designed this course. This stretch of land clearly begged for a golf hole.

It was a perfect length, not too long, easily reachable in one. There was a rock-bound curve on the left border of the fairway. No rough, just a sheer drop. You had to hit directly over the gorge to reach the green. And, oh, the rush of fear as I stood on that tee box, looking out over the valley. Whoever laid out this hole had truly understood the secret of unity.

Player tested the wind. It was gentle but was helping us.

Undaunted by the cliff, he pulled out a two-iron and hit a beautiful shot to the center of the green.

I took a deep breath and pulled a one-iron from my bag. It was more club than Player had used, but I was also tighter than he was. I had a split second of indecision, but then I thought, Trust yourself.

Standing to the side, I completed two practice swings to calm my nerves. I stepped up to the ball, waggled, and swung.

My heart was in my throat. I'd hit the ball fat.

I held my breath as I watched it loft. It flew higher and higher, directly over the gorge. The rocky slope looked like a magnet, drawing my ball down . . . down.

It hit the near edge of the green and bounced cleanly toward the pin. I let out a huge sigh of relief.

Player clapped, and we laughed all the way to the green.

"Why do you always wear black?" I asked.

Player smiled with pleasure. "Clothes are simply another way of influencing body-spirit harmony. Paying attention to your clothes is a mystical metaphor for paying attention to your body. After all," he said, "if you're a being of spirit, your body is simply the clothes you wear."

"But why black?" I questioned. "Does it have something to do with your secret?"

He nodded. "Black captures the energy of the sun and adds to my strength. It's a seemingly insignificant gesture, but it always reminds me that I come from a greater source. When I feel the heat sinking into my body, it reminds me of God. That gives me strength."

I was awed by Player. His almost fanatical adherence to diet and exercise, his black clothes—I'd thought they were all idiosyncrasies. Now I saw the meaning behind the quirks.

AFTER A DAUNTING TEE SHOT, we were rewarded with a large, barely contoured green. Player had hit his iron shot conservatively to the center of the green, and now he carried a cocky putter.

His ball lay thirty-five feet from the hole. He studiously read the green and took his stance. His brow wrinkled in unmoving concentration; his hands and body were perfectly still. Putting for birdie, Player rapped the ball.

It rolled briskly to the hole as if scared to do anything but, and hit the back of the cup to score Player his second consecutive birdie.

My ball was fifteen feet from the cup. I surveyed my lie. It sloped gently downward and slightly left. I stroked the ball, and it began rolling ever so gently. As the ball turned, time seemed to slow. I felt every revolution of the ball as it inched along, slower and slower. Then, just as I'd hoped, it broke. It curved toward the hole, picking up speed as it went.

I groaned in disappointment as it rolled past the hole, stopping two feet away. I tapped in for par.

"Beautiful," Player exclaimed.

"It was only par. I wanted a birdie, like you."

"But Zachary, your par was so much better," he said. "You trusted your intuition with your tee shot and with your putting. That's more important than a hundred birdies. You're learning how to move body and spirit together."

I smiled broadly, proud to have pleased him. Then it suddenly hit me. Player was my competitor. My face dropped. He shouldn't be helping me. Yet here he was, boosting me up. I was sure he wanted to win today as much as I did.

Player laughed, snapping me out of my reverie. "Zachary, your face betrays your thoughts," he said with a chuckle. "Why *wouldn't* I help you? I never pray for victory. Rather, I pray for courage, strength, and guidance.

"Faith is a very important part of my life," he said. "I often think of myself as a missionary. My life is my example. I show others through my achievements what can be done.

"And nothing would make me happier than to see you play your absolute best golf today. Because," he said in a gentle voice, "we're all brothers."

4   *The Secret of Joy*

Tony Lema joined us on the sixth hole.

With his first step onto the course, he swept me back to the era in which he'd lived. He exuded the confidence and hope that I suppose will be forever entwined with the early sixties. That time had been America's youth, as well as my own, a time when we believed in miracles. When I thought perfect golf swings would last forever.

Lema looked like a man of the sixties. He was tall and handsome and tanned. He knew how to dress (conservatively), he knew how to behave (relaxed, but with attentive good manners), and he knew how to think (confidently, but not with cocksureness). Dark hair framed his high forehead, and his eyes glittered like black pearls.

Standing next to Lema, I felt eighteen years old again, and the world was shining with promise. The sun seemed brighter, the sky bluer, and the wind gentler. A feeling of intense joy washed over me, and I was left weak-kneed, clinging to my golf bag.

The last time I'd been this happy was the summer of 1963, the summer of my innocence.

The world then was a buffet of food just waiting for me to eat. I wasn't going to conform to my parents' society. I didn't have to. It was *my* time, my whole generation's time. I remembered cruising to the golf course in my old Dodge Dart, windows rolled down, wind bristling my short blond hair, Jan and Dean's "Surf City" blasting on the radio. John F. Kennedy, Jr., was president. He was young and vibrant, and I knew that with him leading us, the world would be different. Hell, Kennedy even played golf with Hogan irons. If *that* wasn't a sign of perfection, I didn't know what was.

When I cruised in my faded blue Dodge Dart, I felt that I could change the world. I wasn't going to end up in a dead-end corporate job. Not like my dad. I was going to the University of Texas. I used to sing the words to myself: *the U-ni-ver-sity-of-Tex-as.* I was going to play golf, and when I was done there, I was going on tour. No more oppressive winters for me. My dad broke his back every winter shoveling snow. At forty, he was just plain worn out, satisfied just to keep his head above water. Not me. Man, I was going to get *out* of there. I was going to Texas, where the sun shines all year long. I was going to have a life on the golf course, with all the warmth and hope Kennedy had promised me. A life where every weekend brought another tournament and another possibility for a miracle.

Golf wasn't just the game I wanted to play; it was the life I wanted to live.

Pulling myself back to the present, I looked at Gary Player, who smiled at me like the Cheshire Cat. He looked as if he'd known all along that I'd find my innocence with Tony Lema.

In that moment, I wanted to play golf with Tony Lema more than I'd ever wanted anything. I wanted to go back with him to the sixties. I wanted to close my eyes and let this feeling—this innocence—wash over me again and again until it was all that I remembered, all that existed.

Player winked at Lema and then at me. Just for a minute, I wondered if Player had brought Lema back from the dead simply to give me this feeling of perfect golf. Without a word, Player picked up his clubs and played through, leaving me alone with my dream.

I suppose Lema was comfortable with the suddenness with which people appeared—and disappeared—at West Wind. Me, I just watched Player walk off into the distance, gradually turning into particles of infinity, and shook my head in amazement.

"So, Zachary," Lema asked, "how have you been playing today?"

"I'm even," I replied proudly. "You?"

"Three under."

Lema's question was right out of the sixties. He hadn't asked, "What's your score?" but "How have you been playing?" He'd left me an out. If I'd been playing well, I'd say so. If not, I wouldn't have to reveal my actual score. Guys in the early sixties did that sort of thing for one another. I hoped Lema wouldn't notice my loopy grin.

As we walked to the sixth tee box, I felt the magic stirring. I don't know if it was the magic of 1963 or the magic of Tony Lema, but my beautiful rhythm was beginning to come back to me.

The sixth hole was the severest par I'd faced yet. It was a par four, 436 yards. The fairway crested above us with no clear sight of the green. If I smothered or hooked my drive, my ball would vanish in the left-hand screen of fir trees. If I pressed for distance, who knew what hazards lurked beyond the crest of the hill? I'd have to play this one blind. With Lema by my side, I wasn't daunted a bit.

Lema hit first. He had a looping, easy-looking swing. It was, in fact, *so* easy-looking that I forgot to worry about my own. I just loosened myself up and found the rhythm I'd last possessed when I was eighteen.

As we walked toward our second shots, I asked Lema what his life had been like on the pro tour.

"When I played," Lema said with a smile, "Arnold Palmer was king, the first man to really get rich from playing golf. Gary Player was the man in black to beat, and I—well, I was on the knife edge of success. I was one of the best, capable of being *the* best, but also in danger of drifting out of sight." Lema paused to light a cigarette.

He wasn't shy, nor was he boastful. He *had* been one of the best, a tall and handsome playboy with a reputation for daring and largesse. As we strode over the crest of the fairway, the hovering sun sprinkling us with warmth, Lema explained what had lured him—and every other pro golfer—back to the course week after week.

"It was money," he began. "Golfer's gold. Let me draw you a comparison. In 1953, the total PGA purse was $625,000. Back then, you were never going to get rich playing golf. If you were good—really good—you could crank out a living. By the time 1963 rolled around," he continued, taking a long drag on his cigarette, "the purse was over $2.2 million. And I'll tell you, everyone wanted a piece of the gold. Every club pro and every weekend golfer dreamed of making it big on the tour."

Boy, wasn't *that* the truth. I felt my old desire to play on tour rise so acutely within me that it began to itch and nag.

"When you play on tour," he said, "there's a constant riptide of distractions. Your heart is pulled out every weekend for the whole world to see. Your every weakness, your every inadequacy, is laid bare—on TV no less—for millions of people to see. I've seen golfers lead a tournament for three days, just to blow a five-stroke lead on the final round." He blew out a steady stream of smoke. "And then there are the miracles. Anything can happen—and does. There's prize money, and big-money endorsements, and contracts.

"Ah, the thrill of winning. The pleasure of playing in a big tournament is so acute it almost completely wipes out the pain of nervous tension. The tour guys love it, and those who've left itch to come back."

I knew exactly what Lema was talking about. The thrill of a well-placed shot, the elation of the gallery, the certainty of standing alone on the eighteenth green on Sunday afternoon, knowing you were the best. *The best!*

I'd tasted tournament golf as a high school champion. No matter what the price, no matter how naked you might feel on the golf course, the feeling of being the best always lured you back.

I GREW UP LOVING GOLF.

The golf swing—that most unnatural of motions—had seemed like second nature to me. I'd experimented with a flat swing like Ben Hogan's, a classic swing like Jack Nicklaus's, a dancing swing like Byron Nelson's. I discovered myself in that crazy corkscrew motion.

I loved ball-striking. I experimented with everything—opening the clubface, fading a ball, drawing it, punching it high. If I could dream it, I could make it happen.

More important than all that, I found the freedom I longed for on the golf course. On that sparkling field of green, I could be whoever I wanted to be. I could live my life with courage, I could let my feelings show, I could play with aggressiveness or conservatism—whatever I wanted. Golf was a game of magic and of fascination.

WE STOOD AT THE CREST of the fairway surveying our approach shots. We'd hit almost identical drives, and our balls had safely cleared two large fairway bunkers. The silence was companionable. Lema felt like my oldest buddy, my best friend.

"My dad never understood why I wanted to play golf," I said. "He never saw me play. Never bothered to come out and see me win the city championship. That only made me want to play golf all the more."

Lema raised his brows in question.

My voice was dry. "I never wanted to end up like him. The corporate life sucked out his soul. He punched a timecard every day and sat behind a desk pushing paperwork at a job he hated. When he was forty years old, I'd never seen anyone look so ancient. He was absolutely lifeless. He didn't remember what it was like to have a dream anymore."

"Golf was my ticket out, too," Lema said. "My father died when I was three years old, leaving three boys and a girl for my mother to raise. Everyone worked pretty hard in my family. I did everything I could to carry my share of the breadwinning burden." He paused, casting me a mischievous smile. "I also did a little bit of hell-raising on the side."

"Tony, I can't imagine such a thing," I teased.

"Well, thank goodness for golf!" he said. "I began to caddie when I was twelve at the nearby Lake Chabot municipal course. Oh," he sighed, "how I loved to play. I found my independence in golf."

"Just as I did, " I said softly.

Lema looked reflective. "A bad score was entirely my fault, and a good one was entirely to my credit. By my teens, I loved golf so much I played hooky from school just to hit the course." He laughed at the memory. "After high school and a stint in the Marines, I was at loose ends. Once again, golf showed me the way. I applied for a job as an assistant club pro at the San Francisco Golf Club, one of the poshest clubs in the Bay Area. I got it," Lema said. "It was there that I learned how to play golf with a professional flair."

Looking at Lema, I had to agree with his characterization. The tall boy from a working-class family had grown into an immaculately handsome golf pro. The collar of his golf shirt was flipped up just so, and I figured it must have taken him at least ten minutes in front of the mirror to effect that apparently random, seemingly effortless flip. Tony Lema *was* a professional, in every sense of the word.

"I learned how to play golf well enough," he continued, "to qualify for the 1956 U.S. Open in Rochester, New York. A bunch of guys back home got the money together to back me. That Open was my first taste of big-time golf," he said, sighing with happy memories, "and it hooked me like an addict. As soon as I stepped onto the Oak Hill course in Rochester, I felt the spotlight of tournament golf and big-time players. And I wanted to be one of them. I wanted to see if I could make it against the best.

"I was so green," he said, laughing with self-deprecation. "I didn't even know about the cut. That was a bitter little fact of life. The selection process is called 'the cut' quite appropriately, though, because its existence makes you want to draw a knife across your throat from time to time."

I laughed in response. "I feel that way every time I play."

"The beauty of golf," he said, and I agreed.

"How'd you finish?" I asked. "Hagen told me a story about placing second in his first U.S. Open."

"That's Hagen, all right. He'd have told you he won it, if you'd have believed him." Lema laughed. "Myself, I made the cut— barely. I finished second to last and took home a check for $200. I quickly learned that the course I played as Joe Club Member and the course I'd play as Joe Touring Pro were entirely different, even though I'd be treading the same fairway and putting the same greens.

"There's such a thing as cup placement and back tees. The course you play as a pro is 400 to 800 yards longer. There are no preferred lies and no gimmes. The roughs are rougher, and the greens are ironed flat.

"When I have a bad day, I'll shoot a 76 or a 78. Inevitably, some club pro comes out and says to me, 'I shoot 72 here all the time. Perhaps *I* should join the tour.' Well, I tell you, Zachary, it's a tribute to my great restraint that I wasn't booked for manslaughter every other week."

THE ENTRANCE TO THE GREEN was narrow. Trees stood sentinel on either hand, a butterfly-shaped pit of sand spread before it.

I hit a nice conservative mid-iron to the center of the green. Lema was a bit more daring; he aimed for the pin and tucked his ball safely in position for a birdie. What we were doing, though, hardly felt like tournament golf. It felt like a round between buddies.

"So what happened, Zach?" Lema asked. "Why didn't *you* join the tour?"

"I guess *life* happened. You know, a mortgage to pay, a kid to feed."

Lema responded with a soft grunt and shake of his head, as if he didn't quite believe me.

"It was different in the sixties," I explained. "I mean, you know what it was like. What it was *really* like. There was a spark of independence, a feeling that we could do anything. But the spark didn't last forever. Real life has a funny way of intruding on dreams."

"Never let it be forgot," Lema quoted, "there was once a shining spot, for one brief moment, called Camelot."

"You remember!" I exclaimed.

"Yes," he agreed, nodding. "I remember it all. I lived it."

"Kennedy had that record, the Broadway recording of *Camelot*, playing on his record player before he was killed in Dallas. They found it there, still on the turntable, after his death," I recounted.

"Yes, I remember." Lema's voice was very soft.

IT WAS SNOWING AT HOME on the day of Kennedy's inauguration. I sat in front of the television set in Philadelphia, watching the inaugural procession that cold January day in 1960.

Kennedy was so young, so vibrant and enthusiastic in his elegant top hat and tails. He awakened a spark of independence within me and within Tony Lema, too. Of that I had no doubt.

John F. Kennedy, Jr., made us all believe that whatever we dreamed of, we could accomplish. He made me believe in my dreams of a life on the pro golf tour, in my dreams of equality and freedom and independence.

The torch has been passed to a new generation of Americans.

My skin tingled. The torch had been passed to *me*.

All this will not be finished in the first 100 days. Nor will it be finished in the first 1,000 days, nor in the lifetime of this administration, nor even perhaps in our lifetime on this planet. But let us begin.

I'd believed that his idealism and his enthusiasm would last forever.

And so, my fellow Americans: ask not what your country can do for you—ask what you can do for your country.

For the one brief moment that was Camelot, Kennedy had made me believe it could all be different.

"SO YOU NEVER JOINED the tour." Lema's voice held a trace of sadness. My regret penetrated even him.

"No," I said, "I never did."

Lema stroked his ball in for birdie, and I two-putted for par. As we pulled our balls from the cup, Lema looked at me and I saw all my own regrets reflected in his eyes. My flawed golf game lurked just outside this bubble called West Wind, and Tony Lema knew it.

"How about a beer after the round?" I asked, gently changing the subject.

"A beer?" Lema began to laugh uproariously. "Do you know who I am?"

"Sure," I said. "You're Tony Lema."

"I'm *Champagne* Tony Lema."

I screwed my face up in question.

"I drink only champagne after a round," he said, still laughing.

We reached the seventh hole and dropped our golf bags at the tee box.

"The press nicknamed me Champagne Tony in '62. I promised that when I won, I'd buy every last reporter a glass of champagne. Not the cheap stuff either. Moët & Chandon. Only the best for Tony Lema.

"After I made that promise, I started winning . . . and winning big. I won the British Open in '64, and I tell you, the champagne was flowing after that one. I hugged the silver claret jug—that coveted prize—to my chest so tight that people thought they'd have to fill it with champagne to pry it loose from my grip."

Our laughter echoed down the fairway.

"So there's no way I'll meet you for a *beer* after this round. Only champagne," the consummate playboy concluded.

THE SEVENTH HOLE reminded me of Augusta, as it did Lema.

"When I play here, it's like the Masters all over again," Lema said softly. "I just can't get enough of it. It looks so beautiful that I want to lie down and roll around."

I knew how he felt. The grass was a carpet of silky waves in the morning light. It smelled fresh and tangy.

The seventh hole was a gentle par four. It cut softly to the left, with a bunker guarding the outside edge. Each hole on this course was carefully planned, with an eye toward where the tee shot might be placed or the cup might be cut into the green. It didn't so much punish a bad shot as reward a good one.

I chose my club with care, thinking that the process of club selection was one of the great joys of golf. It wasn't like basketball or baseball, where all players used the same equipment. No two golfers played a course the same way. Each found his or her own path to the cup. I might choose a three-wood; Lema might choose an iron. We'd both be right.

"Tell me, Zachary," Lema asked as we lined up our tee shots, "why do you play golf?"

"Why do I play golf?" I repeated. "To shoot the lowest score, I guess."

"No." Lema was firm. "Why do you play?"

"To learn. To improve. To stop making stupid mistakes."

Lema hit a beautiful one-iron, but within his swing I noticed a twinge of irritation. I selected a two-iron and decided to open the face up a little. My ball skidded to a halt just past the fairway bunker.

Lema turned his glittering black gaze directly upon me. "I'm getting really tired of hearing you talk about what's wrong with your game, Zachary. All I hear is *learn, correct, improve.*" He was uncharacteristically pointed. "How does it feel to come back to golf after a long absence? To feel a club in your hands, to just want to waggle that club all day long?"

I nodded stupidly, not quite sure what to make of Lema's mood.

"Pure enjoyment," he concluded. "Think of that word: enjoy-ment." He emphasized the second syllable. "To en*joy* is to give yourself joy. That's what golf is about. To give you joy."

Our footprints made barely a trace upon the fairway as we walked toward the green.

"Golf isn't about scoring the lowest, or getting the right swing, or making long putts, or improving, or correcting. It's about joy. If you've lost your game, Zachary, it's not because you've lost the in-nocence of your youth. It's because you've lost your joy."

I felt an irritating tingle in my nose, a sure sign I was getting mad.

"I KNOW WHAT things were like in the sixties," Lema declared. "I *lived* it, Zachary. I knew hope, and idealism, and dreams."

Lema paused to light a cigarette. He took a long, unabashed drag, the kind people took before they knew cigarettes cause cancer.

"Hell," he continued, "I believed in the vision as much as you did, *more* than you did, because I never gave it up."

I started to protest, but he held up a hand to silence me.

"Zachary, I grew up in Oakland, California. It was a working-class town where people struggled for anything they got out of life.

"I learned golf from a colored golfer. His name was Lucius Bateman, and he could've gone on the pro tour and beaten every last one of us. There was only one problem: the PGA didn't allow colored players back then."

Lema inhaled again, enjoying the knife-cut to his lungs. "Lucius, like other black golfers, earned his living on the driving range, teaching his secrets to white kids like me. When I heard the speech that Martin Luther King, Jr., gave in 1963 on the Capitol steps, I believed in his dream.

"When he said, 'I have a dream that my four children will one day live in a nation where they will not be judged by the color of their skin but by the content of their character,' he spoke to *me*, Zachary. It was personal. I wanted to see the day when Lucius and I could play in the same tournament, his chocolate-colored face next to my honey-colored one. I never gave up hope."

"That was different," I objected.

"Like hell it was." Tony flicked his cigarette with obvious irritation. "If you've lost faith in your golf game, Zachary Tobias, you have no one to blame but yourself."

By now, my nose was itching really bad. I liked Lema; truly I did. But his optimism was getting under my skin. Having died in 1966, he'd felt all of the confidence of the sixties but none of the tumult, and he lived in easy times now. He hadn't had to live through King's death and the Vietnam War and Nixon's disgrace. He hadn't had his hope and faith smashed like last year's Christmas ornament.

Once again, I tried to explain myself. "Haven't you ever hit a slump?"

"A *slump?* Is that what you're calling it? You've been mooning around for the last two holes about how perfect life used to be, and talking about how you couldn't join the tour because of 'real life,' and now you're calling it a *slump?*"

"Hey, just answer the question," I snapped. "Have you ever hit a slump?"

Lema shook his head, and I scratched my nose. This guy just didn't understand the realities of life. Perhaps I'd introduce him to my MasterCharge bill.

"A slump, huh?" Lema's tone was curt. "I had much worse than a slump. I had a two-year slide into the darkest night of golf. There weren't enough women or booze in the whole United States to cheer me up. It was 1959 and 1960." He spat the words out as if the simple remembrance of those years tasted bad.

My ears perked up.

"Let me paint you a picture. My freshman season on the tour was 1958. I won $16,000. I didn't see how I could fail to improve in 1959.

"Well, I changed my grip and my stance to get more trajectory on the ball. But once a player starts to experiment with his game, it becomes almost impossible to get back on an even keel. It's like trying to cut down and even up the legs of a wobbly table.

"During '59 and '60, all the holes began to look dangerous. Every hazard on the course jumped out at me like a flashing neon light. Fairways that had always seemed wide now looked like narrow little paths through fields of wheat. Trouble seemed everywhere."

"What did you do about it?" I asked.

"When I wasn't throwing clubs," he said, "I was giving up at the first sign of bad luck. If I hooked my iron shot, I'd blow a putt just to punish myself. What did it matter? Nothing seemed worth saving. I'd forgotten my first lesson of golf: *joy isn't circumstance-dependent.*

"So when I tell you, Zachary"—he turned his black gaze upon me once again— "that you have no one to blame but yourself, I know what I'm talking about. Joy isn't circumstance-dependent. Golf isn't about what's wrong. It's about what's right."

MY NOSE WAS ON FIRE.

"You don't understand," I said solemnly. I didn't want to argue with Lema, but frankly, I thought he was being a little naive. "Listen, Tony," I began, "I think you're a really super guy."

He started laughing. "Just say what's on your mind."

"You don't know what you're talking about. I mean," I gestured around the course, "this is a pretty perfect place, and you live in pretty perfect times. You have no idea what the real world is like."

"The real world?"

"Yes. The real world. A world where presidents get shot."

"You think I don't know what you're talking about? I lived through Kennedy's assassination. I was playing golf when the announcement was made. I just picked up my ball and walked in. Didn't even finish the round. I've never done that before. I felt the same grief you felt."

"Well, I was in a cold dormitory room at Penn State. I didn't have the *luxury* of being on a golf course."

"Hey, Zachary, I knew tough times."

"No, Tony, you didn't." I was firm now. "You *don't* know what it was like. Sure, you lived through Kennedy's assassination, but let me tell you what tough times really were.

"Even though Kennedy was dead, his spirit lived on, for a while. Jackie was so brave in her blood-spattered suit. Then it all turned to crap." I spit that final word out. "You remember who we got as president after Kennedy: Lyndon Baines Johnson. Well, he started sending my friends, *my friends,* to die in his stupid war in Vietnam. Demonstrators—hundreds of demonstrators—marched outside the White House, singing, 'Hey, hey, LBJ, how many kids did you kill today?'

"It was the same White House where Caroline used to ride her pony on the lawn, and Jackie and John-John used to play tag. Do you know how it felt to see demonstrators taunting the president after we'd known that kind of perfection?

"And then," I laughed sardonically, "we got Nixon. Do you know what it's like to find out that your president—*your president*—is a liar? There's nothing sacred anymore; there's no one you can truly trust.

"You tell me about Martin Luther King, Jr.? Well, I'll tell you what happened to him. Shot. An assassin who didn't like King's vision of a nation without color barriers.

"And the biggest tragedy of them all? Bobby Kennedy. He was our last hope. Do you know what he said?" Tears filled my eyes, and my voice was quaking. "'Some men see things that are, and ask, Why? I see things that never were, and ask, Why not?'" I choked back the memory of Bobby Kennedy's body sprawled on the floor of a California hotel. "Do you know what happened to him? Shot. And all of our dreams died with these men."

I swallowed hard. "It wasn't just me, Tony; it was everyone. We all had to grow up. You take what you can get, and you do the best you can."

"So you decided to grow up, pay the mortgage, and give up your dreams," Lema said softly.

"There wasn't any other choice."

"And so you tolerate presidents who lie to you. Condone cut-throat businessmen by saying, 'Business is business.' Miss seeing your daughter grow up," Lema added gently. "And you call it the real world."

"What else am I supposed to do?"

Lema looked over at me with the saddest eyes I'd ever seen. I saw my own pain and longing mirrored in them. More than anything, for that one moment, I wanted to hide.

It was a long time before either of us spoke again.

The disillusionment of the past thirteen years settled around me, and I wondered if there truly had been another way through that forest of despair. Had I—had we all—settled for less than we should have? I'd decided that if I couldn't have the dream, I'd learn to play the game of life better than anyone else. If there had to be a winner and a loser, then I was damn sure going to be the winner.

I'd made the same compromises as my father. I was now the man in the gray flannel suit. I packed my clothes every Sunday evening and hugged my daughter good-bye on Monday morning. I wasn't there for her school picnics or her parent-teacher conferences. Maybe one day she'd become a golfer. Would I be just like my dad and miss seeing *her* play in the city championship?

I'd made too many compromises. I'd tolerated distance and loneliness and disillusionment because I'd thought there was nothing better. I'd lost my innocence and didn't know where to find it again. Looking over at Tony Lema, at his gently flipped collar and his perfectly tailored pants, I wondered whether his innocence wasn't so much a product of his times as the exercise of a finely tuned muscle. The muscle of happiness.

As I putted out for yet another par, I wondered, If *I* chose happiness, if I chose to be happy in spite of all outer circumstances, would the world rise to greet me? Was life really that simple?

WE STOOD ON THE THRESHOLD of the eighth hole.

A slender fairway sloped toward the green, and I breathed one single word: "How?"

Lema was quiet for a moment as he took a few practice swings with his driver. He teed his ball and then carefully rested his club against his golf bag. He tapped a cigarette out of his pack, lit it, and inhaled deeply. "Usually, we think of what would make us happy, and we go for that," he explained. "Like you, with your golf. You think, If only I could fix my swing, or If only I could sink more long putts. You think *correct, fix, improve.*

"The problem is that you believe you're doing something wrong. As I said earlier, golf isn't about what's wrong. It's about what's right. You don't need a new swing; you need to enjoy the one you have. You don't need to learn new putting techniques; you need to appreciate and make the most of the technique you have.

"It's the same with life. How often do you tally up the items you need for happiness? More money, more time with the kids, a bigger house. Well, the core belief is that you're unhappy. Yet often when people get the very things they want, they're still unhappy.

"You see, Zachary," Lema concluded, taking a long drag, "the happiness comes first. Learn to appreciate your life exactly as it is."

Lema turned and drove the green.

MY DRIVE LANDED close to the green, just in front of two large guarding bunkers. The green was shaped like a slender pear, and it sloped directly down. It would play hot and fast. I pulled out my lob wedge.

"How did you feel about golf when you first started playing?" he asked.

"When I first played golf," I remembered, "I was happy. Every day was an adventure. I had only five clubs, but I made the most of them. I learned that if I opened the face, I'd punch the ball high into the air. If I struck the ball just left of the sweet spot, I'd fade it. I used to feel like Ben Hogan whenever I hit a ball dead straight."

"Zachary," Lema said intently, "that's the way I feel *every time I play.*"

"I feel that way today."

"Well, that's a start."

As I waggled my lob wedge, I remembered the joy of invention again. I pulled my wedge back and punched it.

My ball lofted, and gravity took forever to pull it down. But when it did—oh, when it did!—it bounced directly toward the pin. One, two, three bounces. And then it hit the flagstick; it actually hit the flagstick and bounced four or five yards off.

"Did you see that?" I cried exuberantly. "It hit the flagstick. *I* hit the flagstick!"

Lema laughed with me, shaking his head in amusement. He hit a precise wedge to the center of the green and rapped his putt a foot above the cup. Lema tapped in for par, and I, Zachary Tobias, sank a birdie.

TONY LEMA LEFT ME at the ninth tee box. Before he said good-bye, however, I asked him a question that had been at the back of my mind throughout our play together.

"What kind of car do you drive?"

"Would you like to guess?" Lema asked with a grin.

"A fun car. A really fun car," I guessed. "Perhaps that cherry-red Porsche convertible I saw in front of the club?"

"Now you're starting to catch on!"

5　Interlude

My daughter, still groggy from surgery, gently squeezes my hand. Her fingers are so smooth and vital in contrast to my work-worn hands that it seems utterly impossible that she's the one in the hospital bed instead of me.

"Oh, Daddy," she rebukes, laughing weakly, "you're making this story up."

"No, honey," I say, "I'm not."

She cocks one eyebrow in disbelief.

"West Wind was something I should have told you about a long time ago. Think back to 1976. How old were you then? Six? Seven?"

"I was six. First grade," she says softly.

"Do you remember a business trip of mine out West? I came home in late April, right before your school picnic. We went to it together and won the sack race."

"Wait a minute," she says. "I *do* remember. You got home in time to go with me to the picnic, but it wasn't just that. You were different. You started coming home from work early, playing with me more, and . . . "

I can see the wheels of her memory turning, pulling out old index cards of remembrances.

"That's when you started taking me to the golf course with you on weekends. It was after that trip, wasn't it? In '76?"

I nod, tears welling in my eyes.

"You started taking me to the golf course, and I'd putt with you on the practice green. You made a miniature putter for me. We'd sit on the club porch and drink lemonade until it was dark. But it wasn't just the time you spent with me. *You* were different. All of a sudden, you were so . . ." Her voice trails off as she searches for the right word. "You were so *happy.*"

For just a moment, she looks very far away. She's six years old again, remembering the evenings we spent on the golf course, her small feet taking two steps for every one of mine. Slowly, she comes back to the present day and casts gray-green eyes upon me.

"You mean West Wind is real?"

"Yes, honey," I answer. "West Wind is real."

I KNEW—EVEN BACK THEN when it happened—that I'd have to prove it someday.

Jones had told me that my destiny was somehow linked with the secrets at West Wind and that one day I'd be called upon to share the information. When that day came, I wanted to be prepared. I didn't want to fail again, to miss another opportunity for greatness.

So I started looking for proof almost as soon as I got back home that long-ago April.

I spent a lot of time at the library. This was 1976, remember; there was no Internet, no World Wide Web. I couldn't just switch on the computer. Hell, home computers hadn't even been invented yet. I spent many evenings in the library, trying to unravel the mystery of what had happened to me at West Wind.

First, I made a list—necessarily short—of the facts that I knew were true:

Number 1: Dead players were rendezvousing with living ones. Impossible as this might seem, it was true. I'd seen Jones and Lema there myself. According to the world, they were most definitely dead.

Number 2: West Wind appeared to be of Native American origin. Even though I'd always thought that golf originated in Scotland, I'd seen the distinctive Native American influence at West Wind with my own eyes. The course was located in a remote area of Utah near other Native American historical sites, and it had unmistakable Native American markings—such as bear-claw bunkers.

I decided to go from those facts to information about the course itself. I started by pulling out old issues of *Golf Digest* and *Golf* magazine, thinking that such a great golf course had to be mentioned in a golf publication. I paged through *Golf Digest*'s listing of the top 100 U.S. courses, fully expecting to find West Wind near the top. After all, this course was more challenging than Pebble Beach, more cunning than Oakland Hills, more graceful than Pinehurst No. 2. But not only was there no mention of West Wind, there wasn't a single Utah golf course listed. Well, I'd *played* West Wind, so I knew it was real even if *Golf Digest* didn't.

I considered another research tack. Perhaps the answer to how my mystical match had come into being had something to do with the *land* of West Wind, rather than the course itself. I mean, I'd heard of ghostly happenings—murdered men who continued to haunt the scene of the crime and that sort of thing. None of my golfers had died in Utah, but I considered the possibility of a haunting anyway.

I looked in the history section next. There were quite a few volumes on Utah history in my local library, most of them dealing with the Mormon pilgrimage and Utah's quest for statehood. Judging by the amount of dust I saw, it had been a pretty long time since these books had been consulted.

I finally found a mention of West Wind tucked away in an obscure history reference book. A simple story about a Franciscan priest who'd traveled through Utah in the late eighteenth century mentioned that he'd passed near a Native American village named West Wind.

That one tiny clue led to another, and another, and another, until I'd unraveled the entire story behind the course.

THE DOCUMENTED STORY OF WEST WIND began in 1776, although the course predated that year considerably.

While the white settlers of the newly named United States of America were fighting for their freedom on the Eastern seaboard, two Franciscan priests were leading an expedition through the Western wilderness, an expedition that would pass directly through the Native American land of West Wind.

Fathers Velez de Escalante and Atanasio Dominguez were looking for an overland route to the missions of California. They began their journey in Santa Fe, New Mexico, and traveled nearly 2,000 miles through present-day New Mexico, Colorado, and Utah. They entered Utah from the east, traveling across the Uinta Basin, and crossed the Wasatch Mountains via Diamond Fork.

Father Escalante is quite famous in historical circles. You can find mention of him in any Utah history book and almost any encyclopedia. He was only the second known white man to enter Utah. His travel diaries hold detailed maps—probably the first maps ever drawn of Utah—as well as vivid descriptions of the native plant and animal life. His diaries also provide almost all of the knowledge we now have of Native American life in Utah—dress, lifestyle, and customs.

As Father Escalante traveled overland through the wilderness, he dutifully noted the flora and fauna; and I wondered, as I read excerpts from his accounts in a history of the Southwest, if he knew his diaries would one day have great historical value. In any event, when he reached the Wasatch mountain range of Utah, he encountered a tribe of Native Americans and lived with them for a time. He called the site of the village West Wind, but I would've recognized it from his description alone.

I quickly identified Father Escalante's mountain flora as blue spruce, ponderosa pine, lodgepole pine, Douglas fir, and alpine fir. They were the same trees that had created a frustrating screen for me as I played West Wind, the golf course.

Father Escalante also noted that elk flourished in the mountain climate, and a few moose. Cougars occupied the high-mountain country, he said, and smaller animals proliferated: fur-bearing beaver, mink, marten, weasel, muskrat, badger, fox, and ringtail cat.

Father Escalante wrote eloquently of the animals he'd seen sheltering on the course. When I read his description of them, the hair on my arms stood on end. Many of the smaller animals, such as the fox and badger (he wrote), nestled into the hilly landscape to seek shelter from the ever-present west wind. They dug into the earth, hollowing out a den against the hillscape. A few months later, the animals abandoned their lairs and the earth dried out and became a sandy hollow. Some of the resulting depressions were quite deep—curving nearly three or four feet down—while others were shallow. The Native Americans honored these earth changes as the will of the Great Spirit and made no effort to fill in the huge, trap-like holes.

I knew immediately that Father Escalante had witnessed the origin of the bunkers I'd seen at West Wind. Without a doubt, the village he'd discovered and the golf course I'd played were one and the same ancient Native American land.

NOW THAT I'D PROVED that West Wind was a real place—an actual, tangible Native American village—I began to search for information on the people who'd lived there.

There were three major Native American language groups in North America: Algonquin, Sioux, and Shoshone. The latter was the predominant language in the western part of the United States, particularly in the Great Basin and the Great Plains areas.

Utah is located smack-dab in the middle of the Great Basin—a depression that extends from the Sierra Nevada mountain range in California to the Rocky Mountains. It covers an area of almost 500,000 square miles and includes both mountain peaks and deserts (including, at the region's lowest point, Death Valley).

Life in the Great Basin is hard. The valley floor is salt flats, often as hard as pavement, and the hills are laden with minerals: borax, potash, gold, silver, and tin. There's very little rainfall, and the lack of natural fresh-water sources, in combination with extreme heat, makes farming and irrigation virtually impossible.

The Shoshone tribes that populated this region are divided into two distinct groups, which (curiously) can be distinguished from

one another by what they ate. The Northern Shoshone, who populated Wyoming and Montana, were known as salmon eaters and
bison hunters. Their eating habits were fairly aggressive and war-
like. The Western Shoshone, however, were food gatherers. Their
diet consisted of nuts, berries, roots, and insects. They had a very
simple, peaceful existence.

During the late eighteenth century, many Native Americans,
such as the Plains tribes and even the Northern Shoshone, had
their first encounters with white explorers and settlers. But the
Western Shoshone, I learned, did not. This one small sect of the
Shoshone line had moved high into the mountains to escape the
scorching heat of the desert. Their way of life—a simple foraging
existence—was impossible in the harsh desert. Rather than adapt,
the Western tribes sought land that would support their peaceable
existence.

The Western Shoshone were an ingenious people, focusing all
of their skills on survival. They lived a communal life. Summers
were spent gathering nuts, berries, and roots. (In fact, roots were
such a staple of their diet that the Western Shoshone were often
called "the digger people.") Winters were weathered in subter-
ranean shelters; the people took refuge from the ever-present snow
and ice within the mountains themselves.

Perhaps it was their isolation from the white intruders or their
focus on survival that allowed the Western Shoshone to remain so
pure and untouched by war. Whatever the reason, they remained a
peaceable people. Their philosophy was that one must not fight—
indeed, one must do no harm to anyone—and one must always do
right.

Their creed reminded me, strangely, of Bobby Jones. He'd always said his competitor was not his fellow golfer but the course itself. Was this not the philosophy the Shoshone lived by? Other
tribes and groups weren't their rivals but their brothers and sisters,

so there was no reason for war. Their only challenge was to learn to triumph over the land, to beat the course, to survive.

With these new facts, my heart started beating a little bit faster. Then I discovered the reason that my great golfers had shown up on historical Native American ground.

THE WESTERN SHOSHONE HAD A DEEP belief in immortality.

They believed that the human spirit doesn't die with the body but travels on to the land of the coyote after death. I read an eye-witness account, written in 1861, of a woman who was killed so her spirit could rejoin her recently deceased husband. That woman's belief in, her utter conviction of, the immortality of the spirit was so great that she willingly stepped forward to die, to be with her husband once again.

Death and regeneration were recurrent themes throughout the Western Shoshone tradition. Not only could lovers be reunited in spirit, but great warriors could come back to teach their secrets to younger men.

By now, my heart was racing indeed, and my skin was clammy.

I found a strong shamanistic pattern in the lives of the Western Shoshone who lived at West Wind. Shamans were the medicine men of the tribe, the wind walkers and time travelers whose waking visions and dreams made them the spiritual leaders of the group. Many shamans traveled into the wilderness to experience altered states of consciousness. Their waking visions, as they were called, were an accepted part of life. Tribal members believed that waking visions were unthought dreams and that great spirits gave knowledge and supernatural guidance to people through them.

Since the Western Shoshone believed in waking visions, per-haps what I'd experienced had been just that—a type of shamanistic impression. In a sense, Jones and Hagen and Lema *were* great spirits, champions of the course. And they *had* come back to teach me their secrets.

I flipped to the title page of the history book I was reading, just to make sure that this was indeed a real book. In some hidden part of my soul, I expected the book to disintegrate in my hands, expected the proof I'd discovered to be lost—merely another waking vision, unproven and unreal.

But the book didn't dissolve. It was solid and real and tangible. The dust tickled my nose, and I laughed when it made me sneeze.

I WASN'T THE ONLY WHITE PERSON who'd been to West Wind, as I've said. Father Velez de Escalante had been there exactly 200 years before me. I wondered if he, too, had experienced a waking vision while at West Wind. Had he, like me, called forth great spirits to guide and instruct him?

It took me quite a while to find a copy of Father Escalante's original travel diaries. Apparently, they've been so widely quoted and interpreted that virtually no library carries the original text. Most libraries simply shelve the historical analyses. I finally found an English translation in the hands of a rare-book dealer, and I was quite surprised by what I learned about Father Escalante and his religious sect.

Velez de Escalante was a Christian mystic, a Franciscan priest in a church that's never been particularly comfortable with mysticism. Mysticism, after all, is a direct, inner knowing of God. If an ordinary parishioner could contact the Spirit within, what would that portend for the future of organized religion? You can understand, then, why the church has had to downplay the mystical ecstasies of saints such as Francis of Assisi and Teresa of Avila, lest others follow their example.

But Father Escalante, as part of a wilderness mission in the second half of the eighteenth century, had no bishop or governing body close enough to disapprove of his mystical practices or of his meditation. Thus Father Escalante was free to follow his heart.

In his writings, I met a man who lived the true Franciscan creed. He sought the face of Christ in everyone he met, gently ministering to each person as he would minister to his beloved Jesus. For hours each day, he practiced a sort of Eastern-style meditation, a quieting of the mind in which he didn't so much pray to God as try to experience the Spirit within.

When Father Escalante came upon West Wind, he met a people who believed as he did. He stayed with them, he wrote there, because he had an affinity with them. He felt as if he belonged. That was what I, too, had felt at West Wind. A part of me—an ancient, primordial part of my soul—had come home at last.

Father Escalante wrote of the religion he found among his adopted people, a nature-based Native American tradition grown out of a strong sense of interrelation with the earth. The tribe at West Wind practiced communal rituals and sacred traditions, including a form of sacred "giveaway" that Escalante noted was remarkably similar to his Franciscan vow of charity. When asked or when they saw a need, tribal members lavishly distributed goods and foods to members of other clans, other villages, and even other tribes. This tradition seemed to be tied to deeply held democratic beliefs, the kind of beliefs that in 1776 were also sweeping the eastern half of the country.

The tribe Father Escalante stayed with was remarkably egalitarian. Family lineage was traced through both female and male lines. All were equal at West Wind: male, female, animal, and land. These people believed in stewardship rather than ownership, explaining to Escalante, "How can you buy or sell the sky, or the warmth of the land?"

Father Escalante was obviously a trusted friend of the tribe, because he was privy to many sacred rites. He recounted a ceremony of thanksgiving to the Great Spirit, for example—a ceremony that was held in late summer. He also saw the coming-of-age ceremonies and many medicine rites.

The ritual that intrigued me the most, however, was named simply "throwing the ball." It was a sacred ceremony in which a participant hit a ball with a long stick, thereby "throwing the ball" toward a distant target. The ball's journey toward that target was symbolic of the journey each Shoshone made in life. As obstacles presented themselves along the ball's path, the participant had to negotiate and overcome them. Father Escalante wrote that this rite was the most sacred of all those he witnessed, noting that great spiritual truths were imparted to the participants.

Father Escalante began to play this game, although (he noted ruefully in his diary) he didn't come close to mastering its nuances. He was particularly frustrated, he said, whenever his ball became trapped in the huge pits that had been burrowed out by animals.

All the various threads of thought finally wove themselves into a distinct pattern in my mind.

Father Escalante was playing golf! And we'd both played the same course: West Wind.

6   *The Secret of Attention*

The sun dappled the tee box. The wildflower rough swayed in the breeze, and I was waiting at the ninth hole once again. The breath of the course began to blow and caress me. It was just a slight, two-club pitch coming from the west.

Two men cut the corner to join me, and as they did, the wind gave a low moan of appreciation. Ahhhh. Jack Nicklaus and Arnold Palmer stepped from the pages of history, and the trees rustled with applause.

Time wasn't linear at West Wind. It melted and distorted like a heat haze. The Nicklaus who walked toward me wasn't the Nicklaus I was used to seeing on television.

This Nicklaus was a twenty-two-year-old blockheaded kid. And not in the figurative sense either. Literally. His head seemed to be perfectly square, the shape emphasized by a blockish brush cut.

His pale blond hair rose straight up like the bristles on a porcupine's back, and sideburns framed his face, perfectly completing the sides of the square. He looked like a cartoon character. I could easily imagine pencil squiggles for ears, his bulging frame drawn by a geeky cartoonist sitting at a drafting table.

If I had to use just one word to describe the young Jack Nicklaus who walked toward me, that word would be *fat.*

No way around it: he was fat.

I tried to think of a more appropriate word, but I couldn't. This kid was so *big.* His thighs were thick, and his rear end was enormous. I didn't want to stare, but I couldn't help it. Every time he bent over, I swore his pants groaned with stress.

Looking at Nicklaus on that April morning, I wondered what he was thinking about. Back in 1962, when Nicklaus was young, he wasn't just fat; he was unpopular, too. No matter how talented he was, no one wanted him to beat Arnie Palmer. I couldn't imagine how it felt to have a whole gallery of people rooting for your opponent. No, not just rooting for him, but actively rooting against you.

NICKLAUS NODDED A GREETING and thrust out his right hand to shake hello. He had stubby hands with short, thick fingers. His handshake was just a little too firm, as if he were nervous. His nails were small, wide, and chewed to the quick.

"So," I asked briskly, "how do you think this hole will play?"

Nicklaus squinted down the fairway, thinking.

Arnold Palmer stood to the side, lighting a cigarette. As he shielded his lighter from the wind, I noticed that his fingers were long and elegant, so different from Nicklaus's.

I was embarrassed to have made the telling comparison, so I quickly looked away and busied myself with surveying the hole.

The ninth was a par five. Most par fives test your skill merely on the tee shot and the final approach. The second shot is simply a matter of making forward progress. That wasn't the case here. The fairway had a narrow waist between bunkers and an uncommonly tenacious rough. The winds were whipping it into a test of thought and control.

"I think it'll play shorter than we expect," Nicklaus said finally. Apparently, he'd been pondering my question the whole time.

Nicklaus teed up first, and while he did, Palmer introduced himself to me (as if I hadn't already recognized him). "Hello," he said in his gentle Pennsylvania accent. "I'm Arnold Palmer. I sure am glad you'll be playing with us today."

"Oh, no," I replied. "I'm the one who's glad."

Palmer cast one of his famous Arnie grins at me, and I felt warmed to the core. This man was so gracious and at ease with himself that I couldn't help but understand why the gallery preferred him to Nicklaus.

Palmer gestured at the fairway. "Are you going to play a driver, or try to control it a little better with an iron?" It was as if he really wanted to know my opinion.

I thought about it carefully, and the small, warm feeling in my gut grew a little brighter. "I'm going to play a driver," I concluded. "I've been doing pretty well with it out here."

Palmer nodded. "Me too."

I nodded with him, surprised at the companionship that had quickly arisen between us.

Nicklaus was still lining up his shot. I couldn't believe how incredibly slow he was. He stared at the center of the fairway for a good long minute, cocked his head to the right, and then took his classic low swing. He hit a beautiful long drive, his ball landing safely in the narrow patch of green between the two fairway bunkers.

Palmer was characteristically wild: he hit a hot draw that burned through the fairway onto the left rough. Mine? Well, it wasn't quite as perfectly placed as Nicklaus's shot, but it wasn't quite as bad as Palmer's either.

THE WIND TURNED INTO VOICES as we walked down the fairway.

At first I heard just a low gallery moan. As we walked, however, the wind began to increase its pitch until a soft voice punctuated the whooshing.

"Go get 'em, Arnie."

Startled, I turned to see who had yelled at us.

No one was there. The screen of fir trees still lined the course. No gallery, no bleachers, no ropes lined the course. We were alone.

I kept walking.

"Hey, Fat Boy."

It was a different voice this time, a harsher voice. I felt the sting of the words. I looked around, again seeing no one, but neither Nicklaus nor Palmer seemed to notice.

"Go, Arnie."

"Send that Fat Boy back to Ohio."

"Arnie—Arnie—Arnie!"

"You can do it!"

The voices swirled around us. Dazed, I saw the edges of the fairway shimmer and shift. The rustling of the trees turned into clapping and then wild applause. In an instant, we were surrounded by hundreds of ghostly spectators.

The course quickly became a tournament circus.

The fairway was roped off, and fans pushed at the seams. Everyone was straining to get a glimpse of Arnold Palmer. People were cheering, laughing, cavorting right along with him.

Palmer's steps grew lighter, and Nicklaus's steps grew heavier. As for me, I got nervous.

The wall of people turned the fairway into a narrow alley. I could feel the spectators' breath on my neck and imagined the heat of their disapproval if I were to hit a bad shot.

The gallery strained and cheered like a giant living creature with hundreds of reaching tentacles. I was afraid I was going to faint.

PALMER AND NICKLAUS HAD BOTH outdriven me, so I was the first one to hit in front of our new audience.

Shakily, I took my stance.

I didn't go through my preshot routine or even take a practice swing. I just focused on getting the hell out of there. Fortunately, my swing managed to hold together under the pressure, and I was able to run the ball up about sixty yards from the pin.

Arnie loved the attention. Jack hated it. Of course, if I'd been Nicklaus, I'd have hated it, too. Those crowds really disliked him.

Palmer's drive was only twenty yards shorter than Nicklaus's, but the rough where the ball had landed was deep and he'd caught a bad lie.

The crowd cleared an opening for him to hit.

Palmer seemed perfectly at ease—*more* comfortable, if that was possible, with his army of fans surrounding him. As for me, I felt their heat closing in.

Arnie slashed his ball out.

It was a flyer. It skittered uncontrollably and landed way short of the green.

Nicklaus began his plodding preshot routine. He surveyed his approach, stepped back from it, then stepped forward again. He tugged at his shirt sleeves and pulled down the ribbing of his vest. I was sure he was getting hot.

He bent over his ball and started picking away pine needles from behind it. He was infinitely careful not to move the ball.

"Hurry up, Fat Boy," someone called from the gallery.

Nicklaus froze. I have to give him credit. He never looked up at the offender. When he'd regained his composure, he just kept on picking at the pine needles. He didn't hurry up, and he didn't respond. If the jibe bothered him, he didn't show it.

I'd felt it, though, and my cheeks burned with rejection.

Nicklaus hit a huge approach shot. It sailed over the guarding bunkers, bit the edge of the green, and bounced toward the pin. He was on the green in two.

The gallery was absolutely silent. The spectators didn't cheer for Nicklaus or even acknowledge his skill with applause.

As we approached the green, I realized that my score on this hole didn't really matter. It was a private duel between Nicklaus and Palmer. That insight calmed me enough that I was able to flop my ball onto the green. I was safely there in three.

Palmer stepped up to his third shot. He was a good forty yards short, but the crowd roared nonetheless when he stepped up to his ball. He was known as Arnie to this crowd, not Arnold (and certainly not Palmer). He could slash it right and slash it left, but the crowd believed—no, they *knew*—that Arnie would do it for them. He might have to bounce the ball off Nicklaus's golf bag, but they knew he'd sink his shot somehow.

Arnie hitched up his pants, squinted at the pin, and pulled out a pitching wedge. He looked at the green, which was a beautiful butterfly shape, undulating much as a butterfly's wings flutter, and then swung. Sure enough, as if the crowd had willed it, his ball lofted straight over the pin and flopped onto the green. It bit and rolled perhaps ten feet from the cup.

The crowd hooted: "Go, Arnie, go!"

I was away, and my hands were clammy at the attention. I knew the crowd was wishing my ball away from the hole. Palmer was clearly the favorite; the gallery just didn't want to see anyone else win. How did Nicklaus deal with all this pressure?

I read the green, figured my ball would break left, and took my stance. I was a little too quick and a little too fast: my ball skittered past the hole.

Nicklaus was putting for eagle. As he read the green, I noticed that the white lining of his pants pocket showed when he bent over. He certainly was big. He carefully read the undulations, circling the hole once and then once again.

The crowd was getting restless. I wished Nicklaus would hurry up. How long did he think people were going to be patient with him? Arnie was smoking a cigarette, seemingly unaware of Nicklaus's infuriating precision.

Nicklaus circled the hole yet again. What the hell was he thinking about? It was a thirty-foot eagle putt. Possibly makable, but probably not. If he left it short, he'd still get a birdie. And this was only the ninth hole, for goodness' sake.

Finally, Nicklaus addressed the ball.

A giggle shot through the crowd. Someone started stamping his feet and was quickly joined by another, and then another, until the green rumbled with noise.

Nicklaus backed away.

I didn't know how the hell he blocked out the noise, but he eventually did. He waited a few seconds, stepped up to his putt again, drew back, and rapped the ball. That beautiful white dimpled orb sped toward the hole as if pulled there by a magnet.

Clunk. Nicklaus had an eagle.

Arnie slashed away but came up with only a bird.

I gratefully pocketed a par.

SOMETHING WAS DIFFERENT ABOUT NICKLAUS when he went to place his ball at the tenth hole. He seemed a little slimmer. His hair was longer, too. In fact, the more I concentrated on Nicklaus, the more he seemed to metamorphose. He looked at least ten pounds lighter, and his hair was now worn in a simple above-the-collar cut.

I couldn't ask Nicklaus about it. What was I going to say? "Hey, Jack, you were really fat back on the last hole, but now you look a little lighter. How come?"

I turned my attention back to the game.

The tenth hole was perfectly suited to Nicklaus's game, and I told him so.

Every golfer has a preferred style of play. Hogan, for example, always followed the same pattern. If the cup was left, he came in on the right. If the cup was on top of the green, he came in below. Nicklaus was the same way, except that he liked to play from left to right. He hit beautiful fades and wanted to use them whenever he could.

This hole could've been designed by Nicklaus himself. The most dangerous hazards were on the left, rewarding the golfer who hit a gentle fade.

As we lined up our tee shots, I teased Nicklaus about it. "I should make you give me a stroke on this one. The course is dishing up exactly what you want—a left-to-right hole."

Nicklaus laughed. "Do you think that's a coincidence?"

Actually, I did. But I should've known better. Nothing was a coincidence at West Wind.

The first shot demanded a well-placed driver, just the kind of precision shot of which Nicklaus—and perhaps only Nicklaus—was capable. Driver-range bunkers lurked to the left and iron-range bunkers to the right.

When Nicklaus addressed his ball, I was struck with a wave of awe. He stood over that ball not as a golfer but as its master. It was an almost sacred experience to stand in the presence of such naked confidence.

He took a hard stare down the fairway, cocking his head just slightly to the right. As he did, the impossible happened: his vision and mine melded. For just an instant, I knew what lurked behind the famous face.

His mind was absolutely quiet. It was *beyond* thought; it was complete nothingness. Nicklaus then focused his vision on a precise patch of grass just beyond the right-hand bunker. He stared at it until his peripheral vision closed in and that single patch of grass was magnified. He saw the individual blades of grass bristle in response to his attention. With that picture in his mind, he looked down at the ball and imagined his clubhead striking it. He pictured the ball erupting from a cannon, bursting forth and rising in the distance. The imaginary ball made impact directly atop the patch he'd envisioned. With both the destination and the journey firmly placed in his mind, Nicklaus was ready to hit.

My thoughts hurtled back into my own mind. I heard the distractions Nicklaus hadn't heard. The shuffling of feet. A stray cough. Birds cawing in the distance. The rattle of golf clubs. The ragged breathing of Arnie's ever-present army.

I watched in amazement as Nicklaus, unhearing, waggled his club and swung. His ball arced exactly as he, and I, had envisioned. It landed in precisely the spot Nicklaus had focused his attention on.

"Beautiful shot," Palmer complimented, and then went on to hit a left-curving draw on roughly the same line.

Did he know how Nicklaus had done it? Had he felt the mechanical quiet of Nicklaus's inner mind, as I had?

I stepped up to my ball and tried to emulate Nicklaus, but I gave a poor imitation. I looked down the fairway with as much concentration as I could muster. Damn, I thought. Watch out for that bunker on the left. Keep it straight and hit it hard.

I didn't see the fairway with the same precision Nicklaus had. To me, it was a moonscape of undulations, each hill blending into another. I tried as best I could to aim for a specific spot on the fairway, but when everything blurred together, I settled for a general direction.

As I addressed the ball, I reminded myself, Don't hit it in the bunker. Then I waggled and swung.

"Damn," I blurted. I pulled it, and the ball flew dangerously left.

"To the right. To the right," I coached, gesturing wildly to herd the ball to safety.

Even when it hit the left-hand side of the fairway, even as it was bouncing straight for the bunker, I kept on pleading, "To the *right.*"

My ball plopped into the sand.

"THE BALL GOES where your attention is," Nicklaus offered as we walked toward the offending bunker. "If you tell yourself not to hit it in the sand, you're going to hit it in the sand."

So Nicklaus wasn't a blockhead after all.

"But I was thinking *don't* hit it in the sand," I said.

"Well," he drawled, "that's the same difference. You expected the sand to be a problem, and it was."

"Harrumph," I responded, resorting to the snort of frustration all golfers understand. As Nicklaus laughed with me, I noticed that he looked a little thinner still.

Okay, I thought to myself, think positive. You can get this ball out of the bunker.

When I looked down, my hopes sank. The bunker was three, maybe four feet deep. My ball had melted into the upper-left-hand side of the lip. In order to get over the ball and hit it forward, I'd have to balance myself half in, half out of the bunker.

I tried to take my stance. My left foot was firmly on the edge, but my right foot slid dangerously close to the ball. Damn.

I tried again. I shifted all my weight to the left, to get some traction, and this time I was able to dig the toe of my right foot into the sand. Awkwardly, I tried to balance my weight.

How the hell was I going to advance the ball?

Think positive, I told myself. You can do it.

No, you can't.

The little voices in my head warred against one another.

I took a practice swing and imagined myself blasting the ball up to the green. Right. I'd be lucky just to get it out of the bunker.

I prayed I'd be able to get enough trajectory to clear the edge. I was going to look pretty stupid if the ball hit the top lip and bounced back down.

Oh, well. Here goes nothing.

I swung. It wasn't quite the best sand blast I'd ever seen, but it did clear the bunker.

THE CLUBS REQUIRED for Nicklaus's and Palmer's second shots, and my (I'm ashamed to admit it) third, bespoke the differences in our personalities.

Arnie and I had taken more scenic routes to the green—he by way of the wildflower rough, I by way of the sand. Nicklaus, on the other hand, had kept his eye firmly on the destination. He needed only a pitching wedge to reach the green, while Palmer and I both needed irons.

I flopped my ball about thirty feet from the hole. Palmer did the same, but because he was Arnie, the crowd cheered as if they were at a high school football game.

"Wooh!" they roared.

Palmer tipped his visor in acknowledgment.

Nicklaus took a long time deciding how to play his shot. The green was comparatively small, protected on the right by a multi-fingered bunker. He stood, hands on his hips, glaring at the hole. When he'd made up his mind, he went for it.

He thumped his ball onto the green, and it dribbled just past the pin, six feet to the left. There was only a smattering of applause.

It was terribly hard to watch the gallery's response to Nicklaus. The spectators just didn't take to him. Maybe it was because of his looks, or maybe it was because he was beating Arnie. Whatever the reason for their slight, I felt it like a leaden weight.

Then the jeering started. Someone ran around to the guarding bunker, carrying a sign that read, "Hit it here, Ohio Fats!"

Ironically, Nicklaus had slimmed down so much by now that he couldn't accurately be called fat anymore.

Nicklaus didn't flinch, and my respect for him grew. He was business-like in the face of the gallery's open dislike of him. He marked his putt and patiently waited for Palmer and me to hole out.

Palmer hitched up his pants, grabbed his putter, and quickly read the green. The gallery took a sharp, collective breath as he hunched over his putt. He faced a thirty-, maybe thirty-five-foot birdie putt. He drew back the clubhead and rapped the ball. It shot toward the hole, right on line.

The gallery continued to hold its breath.

It was a huge putt, and it seemed to hold its line. The ball slowed as it neared the hole—slower, and then slower, until it finally ran out of gas just before the cup.

"Ohhhh," the crowd sighed in disappointment.

Palmer slumped, and his ever-expressive face showed his dashed hopes. He clucked to himself and then waved at the gallery as if to say, "We *almost* had it." Then he tapped it in for par.

My own putting was more the type you'd see on the weekends at a public course. I rapped the ball; but unlike Palmer's shot, mine didn't hold the line. I hacked away until I finally got it down in two. Bogey.

When Nicklaus set his ball and picked up his marker, one lone person in the gallery clapped. Nicklaus meticulously read the green, circled the hole once, and then once again. As he stepped up to his birdie putt, I knew he was going to make it.

I suppose it's always that way with great putters. The decision to sink it is made before the club actually strikes the ball. It's that way in life, too. The decision to master something is made long before you step up to the final stroke.

Nicklaus gently pushed the ball, and it hit the back of the cup with a thud.

"How do you do it?" I asked Nicklaus as we walked away from the green, finally summoning up the courage to talk about the insults I'd heard. "How do you keep playing your game in spite of all this?" I gestured at the unfriendly gallery.

"People generally become what they think," he said. "The gallery wants Arnie to win, not me. If I think about them, it'll happen. So I just don't think about it."

He didn't *think* about it? How on earth could you *not* think about the gallery when people were stomping their feet on the ground and crowing at you to lose?

NICKLAUS CONTINUED TO SHRINK. By now, he was a full forty pounds lighter, and everything about him looked more stylish. His hair was a longer, fluffy blond. It drifted just over his ears in seventies-style chic.

I couldn't hold my tongue any longer. "Hey, Jack," I began. "Can I ask you a question?"

"Uh-huh," he murmured, nodding.

"You look, um, a little . . ." How was I going to phrase this? "You look a little . . . "

"Thinner?" he offered.

"Yeah. Thinner. How are you doing it?"

He laughed. "Well, Zach. What you think about comes to pass."

"You mean you're *thinking* yourself thinner?"

"In a manner of speaking. You've seen how the gallery treats me. Hell, even my wife used to call me Fat Boy when we were dating. I got really tired of being called fat, so I started thinking of myself as thin—and, well, you see the results." He shrugged slightly.

Nicklaus's concentration was legendary. I remembered hearing a story about how he quit smoking. He used to smoke a pack a day, maybe more, and then he quit cold turkey. When someone asked him how he did it, he simply said, "I just didn't think about it anymore."

But this . . . this mental slimming was incredible. I was genuinely impressed by the man.

"It's nothing more than you can do," Nicklaus said. "Everything is a product of your thoughts."

WHEN I LOOKED AT NICKLAUS, I saw what we could all be if only we realized our potential. He wasn't really an exceptional man; rather, he was a singular example of what was possible.

Now, I know most of you will disagree with me. After all, Jack Nicklaus has won more major championships than anyone else has even *dreamed* of winning. He's an incredible shot maker and a brilliant strategist. But I met the man, and I'm telling you, he's not a magician or a wizard; he doesn't walk on water. I think of Nicklaus like this: he's not an *extraordinary* human being but an *actualized* one. He's an example of what we can all become.

Most golfers—most people, in fact—fall far short of their potential. It's not because the potential isn't there; it's because something between our ears breaks down. When I looked at Nicklaus, I saw the realized potential of what lurks in the hearts of all people, and I wanted to know how to bring it out in myself.

"It's positive thinking, isn't it?" I asked. "You have a positive attitude, and that makes you confident, right?"

Nicklaus laughed. "Not exactly."

"But positive thinking is part of it, right?"

"There's a big difference between positive thinking and what I do. Most people think a positive attitude will give you more confidence. Then confidence will give you more courage, so you can go out there and do battle. It never occurs to anyone that there doesn't have to be a battle at all."

"But you have to be confident, don't you?"

"Zach, if you spend all your time trying to think positive, you'll make one big assumption: that you're here, and the world is out there. Positive thoughts don't overcome the world. They *create* the world."

"Create?"

"Create," he repeated. "What I do on the golf course isn't special or different. Anyone can do it. I've been saying this for years. Hell, I've even tried to teach it to young golfers coming up on tour. If your reasoning stops with positive thinking, all you're going to do is build confidence. Yeah, that's a good thing, but it's transitory. Positive thinking gets you only so far.

"If you take the rationale one step further and understand that your thoughts create your experience, then it's a whole new game. I heard a golf reporter once say that I could 'will' more good golf than anyone he'd ever seen. That phrase really made an impact on me. He was right. Good golf is something you *will* into being."

I WAS GETTING TO KNOW NICKLAUS in a way the gallery never would. He was an overgrown Boy Scout, eager to help others be the best they could be, and he rushed to tell me more.

"I remember the '66 British Open at Muirfield," Nicklaus said. "Stepping up to the seventeenth, I was tied for the lead. By the final round in any of the major tournaments, down the stretch with two holes left, playing in the final group, the pressure is absolutely paralyzing. The walls felt as if they were closing in on me at Muirfield, and my rhythm felt like lead.

"The seventeenth is a par five, so I knew I had a chance to make something happen if I could just hold it together long enough. I didn't trust my driver worth a darn, so I took two irons to the green. You've never seen a happier man than me when my second shot reached the green.

"I'd already won a U.S. Open, a PGA, and three Masters. I wanted a British. My ambition has always been to be the greatest golfer who ever lived, and I wanted all four majors.

"I had a huge putt left, but I was going to get that ball down in two if I had to scare it into the hole." He laughed softly. "Maybe that's what I did. My hands stayed steady, and that one little bird pushed me ahead by a stroke. I had a tap-in par at eighteen and won my first British Open."

I HAD MY OWN MEMORIES of Nicklaus, of the early gestures that showed the kindly spirit I'd met at West Wind. One such memory was his first Ryder Cup, the one tournament played not for money but for honor. It was 1969, and Nicklaus was paired against Tony Jacklin—the new British Open champion versus the leading golfer of the age. The team score was tied at fifteen and a half, and the match was dead even as each of them drove off the final par-five eighteenth tee. Possession of the Ryder Cup had come down to this last hole and these last two men.

Nicklaus hit his fairway shot first, finishing thirty feet from the hole in the front rough. Jacklin's ball ran onto the back edge of the green.

Nicklaus chipped his third shot onto the green, while Jacklin putted for eagle.

The crowd surrounding the eighteenth at Royal Birkdale in England numbered 20,000, and Jacklin was the favorite.

The gallery held its breath as Jacklin took his stance. He stroked the ball, but it dribbled to a halt eighteen inches short.

Nicklaus took his fourth shot, putting for birdie. He crouched over the ball and, with a steely will, holed his putt. Then he did the unexpected: he picked up Jacklin's marker and conceded the final stroke.

The match was halved; the final score tied at sixteen all. The Ryder Cup, having been won by the U.S. team in '67, stayed with the Americans, but I was forever impressed with Jack Nicklaus's gracious gesture.

TO BE JACK NICKLAUS is to believe that being human is a grand experience.

He told me that he likened his thoughts to a magnet. Whatever you think about, he told me, attracts energy—eventually enough energy and enough power to come into being. That's how he "willed" his good golf shots. He thought about them so hard that he created them.

The secret I learned from Nicklaus was liberating and terrifying at the same time. Think about it. Our thoughts create reality. If it's an ugly world, that's because we've thought it into being. Conversely, if there are opportunities and kindness and beauty in the world, it's because we've thought of them.

That day at West Wind, I learned that there's a grander purpose to life than simply working at a job, earning a good living, and having a comfortable retirement. We're here to learn how to create. Nicklaus had mastered perhaps the toughest lesson of them all. He'd accepted the ultimate, and very personal, responsibility that every thought, every millisecond of brain power, created his own reality.

As he explained it to me, "It's not so much that your thoughts instantly come to life. If a fleeting thought about breaking your putter flits over the transom, it's not as if your putter will snap in two of its own accord.

"Life is a continuing process of mind over matter. So many times, there will be a mental barrier, an achievement of which no one can conceive. In the 1900s, it was a golf score in the sixties.

Someone dared to think it. He dared to believe it was possible, and so he created it."

SUNLIGHT STREAMED THROUGH THE MOUNTAIN PINES. The day was maturing, dispersing the morning mist and moving gradually into warmth.

"Jack?" I asked.

"Hmmm?"

"Can I ask you another question?"

"Sure." His voice was earnest.

"Thoughts create reality, right?"

"Yes," he agreed, drawing out the syllable as if it were a long word.

"Well, then, what can you create?"

"Anything."

"Anything?"

Nicklaus chuckled. "What are you getting at, Zach?"

I took a deep breath. I remembered how I'd felt with Player and with Lema. Everything I wanted in life was reflected on the course. Hope. Courage. Confidence. I suppose it was evidence of my own version of a midlife crisis that I looked for the answers to life on a golf course; but nonetheless, I knew that when I'd mastered this game, I would have mastered life as well.

When I became an adult, it was as if I lost parts of myself along the way. My belief in the power of dreams was replaced with a sense of limitation and a lack of control. I was a fully socialized adult, but now, playing here at West Wind, I wasn't quite so sure I had to be.

"I'm starting to see possibilities," I said. "Everything—you, the course, the game—it's opening my eyes to a different way of living. A different way of looking at life."

"Uh-huh." Nicklaus nodded at me to continue.

"Well, if what you're saying is true—if thoughts create reality—does that mean I can create a *different* life for myself? If I'm unhappy with something, can I *think* it different?"

"Yes."

"Yes?"

Nicklaus laughed again. "Anything you can dream of, you can have. It might take a little time. You might have to really focus on it, but you can have it. How do you think I became a golf champion? I focused on that goal, giving it the emotional power and kick to come to life. That's the secret of attention."

He paused a minute to gather his thoughts. "Few people thrive under conformity and sacrifice and compromise, Zach. The way we play at West Wind is about honoring the spirit. There's a time for each lesson—a divine flow, if you will. There are times when chaos is at work, or unity, or joy.

"But you know, Zach, my favorite lesson is attention. If you can dream it, you can do it."

Through the pine trees, I spied Byron Nelson holing out on the fourteenth. Before I left Nicklaus, however, there was one last thing I wanted to know about him.

He'd acted like a champion even when the gallery hadn't treated him like one. He'd never disparaged Palmer or blamed the gallery. Now, standing next to Nicklaus at West Wind, I wanted to know how he really felt.

"Does it ever bother you that the gallery dislikes you so much?" I asked. "That Arnie always gets so much more attention?"

He thought about my question carefully. "Some days it does," he finally said. "I think that no matter what I do, the crowds are always going to like Arnie better than me. But then," he added with a grin, "I'm going to win more tournaments."

7 The Secret of Integrity

My shot on the fifteenth wasn't supposed to happen. I'd learned how to focus my thoughts. I was supposed to be getting *better,* not worse.

Disaster met me when I rushed toward Byron Nelson on the fifteenth tee, eager to show off my new skill.

"Mr. Nelson," I called out, waving at him. "Can I play a few holes with you?"

He waved back and motioned for me to join him. I jogged across the adjoining fairway and watched as he teed up.

"Where's Mr. Hagen?" I asked, remembering that Hagen and Nelson had been paired together.

"Oh, I sent him on his way," Nelson explained, "so that you and I could have a little time to ourselves."

Sure enough, I looked down the fairway and saw the misty, almost transparent figure of Walter Hagen playing through. He was gesturing to a now-invisible gallery, tipping his cap and waving in an exaggerated pantomime. Hagen was, and would always be, the great showman.

Nelson and I settled in to play. I was focused not on what I could learn but on how I could show off. That, I suppose, was my first mistake.

The fifteenth was a long par four with a pinched-in landing area. We both needed a driver, that much was certain, but we also needed accuracy. The fairway was a steady climb to a crowned landing area, guarded on the left by an arrowhead bunker and punctuated on the right by a deep ditch.

Nelson hit first. His swing was unorthodox, with a distinctive rocking motion to it. He hit the ball solidly and straight, however.

I tried to thread my ball to keep it in the middle, but I opened up the clubface just a little too much and sliced it instead. I grimaced as my ball flew into the right-hand ditch.

Damn. If I screwed this hole up, that would be two bogeys in a row. Not the kind of play I wanted to show Byron Nelson. I wanted him to see how much I'd improved since we'd first teed off that morning.

I resolved to get down in two and save the hole. There was just one little problem: I couldn't find my ball. My cheeks burned with shame as I searched through the ditch. Nelson came over to help me, which only underscored my embarrassment.

"It's got to be here somewheres," he said in a liquid Texas drawl.

"Harrumph," I snorted, my frustration growing by the minute.

Finally, I gave up and walked back to the tee box to reshoot. It was the loneliest 200 yards I'd ever walked. I felt like a Death Row inmate taking his last walk, straight to the electric chair. My steps thudded, and I figured nothing could be worse than this pillory.

I was much less cocky on my second drive, now that I was hitting three. My ball landed way short of Nelson's, but I was grateful that it at least hit the fairway where I could find it.

My fourth shot reached the green, as did Nelson's second.

He tried to soothe my anger over having lost two strokes. "You know, Zachary," he said, "sometimes you've just got to hang in there. A lot of golf is attitude. If you learn what you're supposed to learn from each shot, then you're doing okay." His drawl was so languid that *okay* sounded like a four-syllable word.

Nelson was by far the most talkative golfer of the group. He gave me advice as we read the green, then clucked in sympathy when my first putt missed the hole. As he lined up his own putt, he told me what he was doing.

"Everybody's got an individual putting style," he said. "Me? I just try to keep still. I'm not as *pretty*-looking as some of the other golfers, but I get the job done."

He was putting for birdie. Needing a good twenty-footer, he stroked the ball right on line but left it three feet short.

"You see?" he said, laughing. "Even I'm not perfect."

He tapped in for par, while I stepped up for my own double-bogey putt.

I wish I could say that I skillfully stroked my ball home. Perhaps if I were making this story up I would. I'd say I stepped up to that ball as if I were its master and popped it in the cup. But I didn't. My lousy putting continued, and so did my embarrassment at playing like a rank amateur.

I managed to three-putt the hole and take a seven.

A triple bogey.

"ARGH!" I SCREAMED IN FRUSTRATION.

I grabbed my putter with both hands and tapped it against my bended knee in a mock-display of breaking it in half. The only thing that stopped me from actually snapping the accursed thing in two was the thought of having to putt the rest of my round with a wedge.

Nelson looked at me intently and then startled me by saying, "Throw it at the tree."

"What?"

"Throw your putter at the tree," he repeated.

It sounded absolutely crazy, but every other guy on the course today had been pretty instructive, so I took his advice. Looking down at that putter, that infernal three-putting instrument, I felt my frustration build once again. With all my might, I pitched it at the nearest fir tree.

It wobbled in the air, twisted round and round, and banged into the tree branches. It stuck there, too, dangling crazily in the middle of the tree. Nelson laughed, a low belly chuckle.

I was embarrassed. As my rage dissipated, I was suddenly ashamed at my behavior.

"Why'd you tell me to do that?"

"Because," Nelson sputtered out between laughs, "that's the only way you're going to learn not to let your frustration get the better of you."

I had to act like a fool in front of a man I wanted to impress in order to learn that?

"I wasn't always so even-tempered myself. One time, back in '36, I did exactly the same thing."

"You?"

"I'd been playing my irons beautifully but not putting particularly well. In my last round, I hit the first five greens in a row, never farther than ten feet from the pin, and I never made a single putt. Well, something just flashed over me, and I threw my putter up in some big old evergreen tree back of the green." He laughed at the memory, and I had to admit that the thought of

Byron Nelson pitching his putter was pretty comical. "I thought that putter was never going to come back down."

By now, Nelson was in stitches. "Just . . . just . . . like yours!"

There's one hazard that hasn't changed since golf originated: a player's temper. I hadn't controlled mine, and now I looked stupid.

I went over to the tree and tried to pull the putter down. It hung in the branches about eight feet from the ground. I jumped but couldn't reach it. My jumping and grasping only made Nelson laugh harder. Finally, I had to climb up into the tree and shake my putter down.

It hit the ground with a thud, as if to say, "Golf either builds or reveals a man's character." My bad behavior had certainly revealed mine.

As we cut the corner to the next hole, Nelson asked how I'd found West Wind.

I knew what he was getting at. West Wind wasn't just a golf course; it was a classroom. More than any other golf course I'd been on, West Wind rose up to teach me the lessons I most needed to learn. Nelson wanted to know the inner journey that had brought me here, and I tried to explain.

"I'm looking for something I lost a long time ago," I said. "You'll probably laugh when I tell you."

"You've got nothing to be ashamed of," he said. "We're all looking for one thing or another on the golf course."

"Well," I said, "I'd better start at the beginning. When I was eighteen, I was a pretty good golfer."

Nelson leaned against his golf bag. Looking at his freshly scrubbed Texas face, I felt that I could tell him just about anything. He had an earnest, heartfelt look about him.

"Go on, Zachary," he said.

"I had a chance to play college golf, but I let myself get talked out of it. I went to a school that specialized in engineering instead."

"I've known a lot of nice engineers," he offered.

"Me too, but I'm not one of them. I was really unhappy there; I didn't fit in. So I dropped out and took a sales job. I was just a detail-man back then. I was the guy who went around to all the drugstores and stocked the shampoo and shaving cream and stuff like that."

"Hmmm." Nelson nodded.

I was proud of how quickly I'd risen through the ranks, and I recounted my accomplishments. "I was the number-one detail-man that first year. I got my own territory, and then a larger one. Now I'm a national sales trainer. I fly all over the country and train other salespeople. Somewhere along the way, I got married and started a family."

"Did you also play golf?" he asked.

"That's the thing. When I was twenty-three, I stopped. Golf just hurt too much. Do you know what I mean?"

"Every time you played, you wondered if you could have been something more," Nelson said. There was no question in his voice.

"Yes. I wondered if I hadn't given up my dream of being a pro golfer too easily. And then, once that little doubt was there . . ."

"It started eating away at you," he finished.

I nodded. "It ate away until one day I just gave the game up altogether."

"But you're here today?"

"Well, five years ago, a client invited me to play golf with him. As soon as I stepped onto the course, I knew I could never be away from the game again, no matter how many doubts I had. That club felt so good in my hands. It was as if swinging it were something I was meant to do."

"And now?"

"Well," I said, "now I've got adult-sized problems. I'm away from my family more than I should be. I worry about money more than I ought to. I play golf a whole lot worse than I'm capable of. I still wonder whether I gave up my dreams too easily. Only now, instead of being twenty and wondering, I'm thirty-one and wondering.

"Every time I play, I have one goal: to play the perfect round. I figure if I can do that—nail my drives and two-putt every green—somehow everything else in my life will fall into line, too."

Nelson chuckled.

"I *knew* you'd laugh!"

"Oh, Zachary, I'm not laughing at you. I'm laughing at the irony of this little game. Everyone secretly believes golf holds the answers to life. That's why we all get hooked on the game so quickly and so deeply. Most people will never admit it, though."

"So I'm not crazy?"

"Not at all."

We paused for a minute, and I let the breeze of the golf course wrap around me like warm arms, comforting me.

"So what are the problems you want to work out?" he asked. "You said if you could play perfect golf, everything else would be all right, too."

It was time for me to tell the truth. I took a deep breath and began. "My problem is compromise. I've compromised everything important in my life. I wanted to play professional golf, but I let my parents talk me out of it. I want to spend more time with my family now, but my job keeps me on the road."

"A man can get mighty lonely if he's compromising all the time."

"Tell me about it," I agreed. "It's like I've taken my heart out and set it on a shelf and said, 'You just wait there a while. I'll get to you later.' And then I go about my life doing everything everyone else wants me to do. There's no time for me to do what *I* want to do."

"And what's that?"

"If I knew, I guess it would be easier," I said dejectedly. "I really don't know. All I know is that life is meant to be more than what I'm experiencing. There's a deeper meaning to everything, but I'm just passing time, earning a living and paying the mortgage."

Nelson nodded as if he understood.

"The guys I've played with so far—Hagen, Player, Lema, Nicklaus—they've opened my eyes to a new way of living. They've made me think that maybe I don't have to do the things everyone else does. But I don't know what I want to do. Everyone here seems to have a destiny. I want to find out what *mine* is."

"I'm sure I can help," Nelson said confidently. "We'll just talk and play, and I'm sure something will come up. After all," he said with a grin, "this is West Wind."

"I want to share a little story with you, Zachary," Nelson said as we began our preshot routines.

Nelson's stories, I later realized, were like Aesop's fables. Each one held a pearl of wisdom and a clue to the real reason I'd been drawn to West Wind.

"My very first official win was the 1936 Metropolitan Open," Nelson said. "It was right after the Met Open that I had my first opportunity to do an endorsement. The company that made a cigarette called 20 Grand asked me if I'd do an ad for them."

"I didn't know you smoked," I said, shocked at the prospect.

"I *don't* smoke," he said. "In fact, I don't believe in it. No one in the Nelson family has *ever* smoked. My parents never asked me to promise that I wouldn't; it was simply a matter of family pride as well as health with me. I knew that to play well, I had to be in the best possible condition at all times."

"Did you take the endorsement?"

"I'm ashamed to say I did," Nelson said, clucking in disapproval. "To be truthful, I wasn't comfortable doing the ad at all, but even with the money from the Met Open, we were really struggling financially. So I said I would."

"You know, Mr. Nelson," I said soothingly, "sometimes you have to do certain things to make a living."

Nelson looked up at me sharply. "No, Zachary, that's where you're wrong."

I was a little taken aback. Nelson wasn't usually this definitive.

"You have to live by your principles. When the pressure is on, how someone reacts shows the inner person, and I'm ashamed to say that taking that cigarette endorsement showed that I had a lot to learn about being a man. Now, I didn't smoke in the ad or even say that I smoked. I just said I'd read a report saying that these cigarettes were low in tar, and so forth.

"As soon as that ad appeared, I began getting letters from Sunday school teachers and all sorts of people, telling me how I'd let them down. They pointed out that young people really looked up to me, and here I was more or less saying that smoking was all right. It really upset me."

"What did you do?"

"I talked to the 20 Grand people and told them I'd give the money back if they'd stop the ad. I promised the good Lord that if he'd forgive me, I'd try to set a good example, never let anyone else down. I've worked very hard at doing that."

"Did they stop running the ad?"

"No," Nelson admitted. "They either couldn't or wouldn't, and I was very sorry about that. But it was an important lesson for me to learn. I never again did something that went against my principles just to make money."

Nelson's lesson got me thinking.

I supposed I hadn't been completely honest when I'd told Nelson what had brought me to the course. He'd asked what my problems in life were, and I'd told him they were just normal adult-sized problems. Well, I guess we all have things in our life we're not proud of—times when we've cheated, for example, or tolerated someone else's cheating. Now, having heard Byron Nelson's own confession, I was suddenly aware of my own failings of character, and I was ashamed of them.

"But isn't it okay," I asked, "to do something you know is wrong if you do it to earn a living for your family?"

Nelson's face told me exactly what he thought about my rationale. He had the kind of face that showed every emotion. When he was happy, he beamed like a ray of sunshine. When he was disappointed, as he was now, his eyes and cheeks and even chin drooped with his dashed hopes.

"Do you want to tell me about it?" he asked.

I didn't, but I figured I needed to. "Right before my company sent me out here, I got a really big order. An order so big that it qualified me for a promotion. But," I continued, taking a deep breath for courage, "I don't really think I should have taken the order."

"Was it a real order?"

"Yes—oh, yes," I said quickly. "It was real. It's just that I don't think my customer should have placed such a big order."

"Well, presumably he wanted to."

"You don't understand, Mr. Nelson." Somehow it didn't seem right to call him by his first name, at least not when I was confessing a character flaw. "This customer really likes me. I like him, too.

I helped him put on a few special promotions when he first opened his chain of drugstores. He wanted to help me out in return, and he knew what a really big order would do for my career. But he doesn't need that much merchandise. I know there's no way he can move it all."

"Hmmm," Nelson said. "I see your problem."

"There's more, though—the other side. I figure that in a few months, after my promotion goes through, he's just going to return the extra stock. Nobody'll get hurt. I deserve the promotion." I was starting to get defensive. "My company will be able to resell the stock to another store. My customer will move some of it."

"But is it *right?*" Nelson asked quietly.

I thought about it for a long time, even though I already knew the answer. "No," I said. "It's not right."

"WHEN YOU CHEAT IN GOLF, the only person you're cheating is yourself." This was Byron Nelson's unforgettable advice to me. He didn't mean only on the golf course, though; he meant off it as well.

Golf is like life in that it gives you a chance to develop character. Facing a difficult shot gives you a chance to build courage. Facing my own inadequacies, just like standing in a bunker, gave me an opportunity to be principled.

Character isn't given to you. It's the hard-won result of making difficult choices in life. Character develops from putting your own gratification second in service of a larger goal.

As much as I'd been wanting to find the deeper meaning in life, somehow I'd never connected my own behavior with my quest. Byron Nelson showed me something different. He didn't show me the easier path; he showed me the only path to spiritual fulfillment.

In his easygoing southern way, Nelson continued to tell me stories about his life. Each one was designed to teach me a lesson in integrity, to point me toward my destiny.

"I'M KIND OF HUNGRY," he said. "How about a lunch like I used to eat in the old days?" He looked eager to share his memories with me.

I nodded. Anything Byron Nelson wanted to do, I wanted to do, too.

"You wait right here," he said. "I'll get it."

Nelson walked off past a cluster of evergreens. I couldn't see what he was doing, but I smelled it. Maybe a concession stand popped up out of nowhere; maybe he pulled our lunch from thin air. However he created it, I smelled it. The aroma of fresh hot dogs made my mouth water.

He came back with two loaded dogs, a couple bottles of Coca-Cola, and a brown paper bag.

"Hot dogs?" Though I'd already identified the smell, I was surprised. "Didn't you eat in the club in the old days?" Somehow I'd always figured stars like Byron Nelson sat down to lunch and ate on tables with tablecloths, china, and silverware.

Nelson laughed at me. "Back in the early thirties, golf pros weren't always allowed to eat in the dining room. That was for members. We were lucky we got to use the locker room. Back when Hagen played, they couldn't even do that."

He handed me a hot dog covered with mustard and relish, and we sat on the edge of the fairway.

"When Hagen played in the early twenties, and even before then, touring pros were really looked down on. Now, I'm not saying if that was right or if it was wrong, but it really stuck in Hagen's craw that he couldn't change clothes in the members' locker room or eat in the dining room. He made a big fuss about it, and eventually golf pros were allowed to use the locker room.

"Change happens kind of gradually, though, even if Walter's kicking up a fuss. By the time I came on tour in the thirties, we could use the locker room. Sometimes we could eat lunch in the dining room, but more often than not we had to fend for ourselves.

"Now, Augusta was the exception. That was Bob Jones's club. He always gave us free run of the place. We could go wherever we wanted—in the dining room, the club room, the locker room. Then again, we were Bob's *friends*, so I think he understood how bad it made some of us feel to be segregated."

As I said, Nelson was a talkative fellow. He just bubbled away, sharing stories and memories, seemingly enjoying my company as much as I enjoyed his.

I took a sip of my drink and remembered how delicious it was to drink Coca-Cola from a glass bottle. Nelson called it Co-Cola, and I smiled to myself at his Texas twang. I took another good, long swig. It gurgled at me, sweet and brown. I'd almost forgotten about the last little bit of sweet syrup that clings to the lip of the bottle. Almost, but not quite. I flicked my tongue across the top of the bottle in enjoyment.

"So did you always eat on the side of the course like this?" I asked.

"Oh, no," Nelson explained. "Sometimes I ate in the locker room; sometimes I'd go into the club lounge. You have to remember, I played golf in the thirties. It was the Depression. I didn't always have the money to eat a fancy lunch. Hot dogs and Co-Cola were just fine with me."

He rustled the brown paper bag he'd brought over with him and pulled out dessert. When I saw what he had, my heart nearly skipped a beat with delight. I hadn't seen one of those since I was a kid.

"Rice Krispie treat?" he offered.

"I'd *love* one," I said, taking the gooey marshmallow-and-cereal bar from his hand. I tore off a corner and let it melt in my mouth.

"My wife, Louise, used to make these for me," Nelson said with a wistful smile. "She was a good woman, and I was lucky to be married to her. She knitted these for me, too." He pulled up a pants leg to show off his argyle socks. "They're one of two pairs she knitted for me when I first went out on tour. They were the only good golf socks I had back then."

"You had only two pairs of socks?"

"Yep. I washed one pair out at night and wore the other pair the next day, because it took them nearly a day to dry." He chuckled at the memory.

I laughed with him and got a mental picture of a young Byron Nelson, rising golf champion, washing out his socks at night so he'd always have a clean pair to wear.

"That was just another part of the Depression," he said. "We made do with what we had. Life's not like that now, and I sure am glad I grew up when I did. The Depression taught me lessons about hard work—lessons I sometimes think young pros are missing."

"What do you mean?" I asked, fully aware that I could have been one of the young pros he was now talking about.

"Well, don't get me wrong," he drawled. "Most youngsters on the tour have a lot of talent—probably more talent than I ever had." Byron Nelson was nothing if not modest. "But hard work builds character. And believe me, you need character to win golf tournaments. Washing out those socks every night helped me remember what's important in life. It didn't matter how many socks I had, or who washed them; it mattered that I was working hard to achieve my dream."

Suddenly, the carbonation in my Coca-Cola tickled my nose, and admiration for Byron Nelson tickled my gut.

I FIGURED I COULD even out my horrendous triple bogey with a birdie on the par-three sixteenth.

"One-ninety-one to the green," Nelson said, as he pulled his three-iron from his bag.

"Looks more like one-eighty to me."

"Nope. One-ninety-one. A little knack of mine is being able to judge distances by eye," he said confidently. "I've heard people say about me, 'He might miss a shot every now and then, but he won't ever misclub.'"

So far I hadn't seen Nelson misclub, but I was hot after a birdie.

The green was crowned, with a dangerous back-right to front-left slope. The cup was cut up top, and I didn't want to overshoot the green and get my ball on the wrong side of the slope, so I ignored Nelson's advice and pulled out my four-iron.

Nelson was up. He took that beautiful rocking swing that was so original and so deadly. His timing was perfect, and his club stayed on line longer than any swing I'd ever seen.

Whomp! He made impact with the ball and sent it cascading toward the hole. He was perfectly on target, landing the ball about four feet under the hole.

Since that April day, I've had time to reflect on my play with Byron Nelson. If he were on tour now, perhaps the television commentators would get bored with him. There wasn't much to announce. He hit every fairway and every green. But was he boring to me? Too methodical? No. There was a natural rhythm to his moves, and I sensed that Nelson played the game the way it was meant to be played.

I hung onto my four-iron out of stubbornness, even though I'd secretly concluded that a three was probably the better choice. You'd think by now I'd have started learning to trust the journey of West Wind and concentrating on the lesson at hand. I wasn't playing with intuition; I was being bull-headed. Sometimes I've just got to learn things the hard way.

Sure enough, I plunked my ball about twenty yards short of the hole in the front rough. Well, I consoled myself, at least I didn't overshoot.

Nelson chatted all the way to the green. In between putts, he kept right on talking, too. He was just so friendly that he couldn't contain himself.

"In my entire career," he said, "I've never asked a caddie what club to use. I'm pretty proud of that. Judgment of distance is a skill, and it's probably one of the reasons I played as well as I did on tour. I always picked the right club."

Nelson didn't mean to rub it in—he was trying to minimize my mistake—but I felt a little sting nonetheless. Judgment is never so harsh as when we inflict it on ourselves.

I slammed my club into my bag and took off walking.

A fuzzy red fox strutted out onto the course, and he stopped to look at us just as we stopped to look at him.

"Hello, little foxie," Nelson called. "Come to play with us today?"

The fox pranced across the course as if to say, "Not today. Perhaps another time," and he flicked his tail in salute.

My nerves were soothed a little bit as I forgot my misclubbing and remembered the course. Gratefully, I chipped my ball onto the green, in line with Nelson's. When we looked at the two balls, we saw that Nelson's was about a half-inch farther from the cup, with my ball resting eight inches to the left of his.

I didn't bother to mark my ball; I just stood aside to let Nelson putt. Nelson read the green, and when he stepped up to his putt, his foot just grazed my ball. He stopped abruptly.

"Oh, no," he said. "I nudged your ball."

"I should've marked it," I replied quickly. "Go ahead and putt."

"I've got to call a penalty on myself. This one'll be for par."

"No," I said. "It's my fault. I should've marked my ball. Go ahead and putt for birdie."

It wasn't like Nelson to stare at me directly, but this time he did. "No," he said, his words distinct. "I've got to call a penalty on myself."

His tone said, "Don't mess with me," so I shut up.

"Let me tell you what happened in the '41 PGA Championship, and you'll understand why. Back then, the PGA was match play. To get to the finals, you had to survive a whole gauntlet of players." Nelson always told a good story, and he always—*always*—started at the beginning.

He continued: "I had to beat the likes of Bill Heinlein, Ralph Guldahl, Ben Hogan, and Gene Sarazen—just to get a crack at Vic Ghezzi, a wonderful player. Against Vic, I was leading three up with nine holes to go when the adrenaline just flowed out of my body. I didn't have any gas in the tank, and it showed. Vic caught me at the end of regulation, forcing a sudden-death playoff.

"On the second playoff hole, we both hit our chips about four feet past the hole. Just like you and me. Well, I accidentally nudged Vic's ball with my foot, moving it about an inch.

"In match play, a violation like that means that you lose the hole, so I conceded the match and the championship. Vic didn't want to win that way, so he told me to go ahead and putt. The PGA official agreed with him, but I didn't. I knew I'd lost by the rules. I felt awfully bad about putting, but I did. And do you know what? I missed that putt and lost the match."

"Did you miss on purpose?"

"No, I didn't. Stepping up to the ball, I realized that if I sank my putt and Vic missed his, I'd win. For that reason, my heart wasn't really in the putt. I'd lost that match when I nudged his ball, and I knew it.

"Later on, I realized the lesson. If you don't play by the rules, you're going to penalize yourself, in some way or another. You're either going to do it up front by taking the penalty stroke, or your conscience is going to do it for you by messing up your next shot."

I thought about it and realized Nelson was right. We *do* penalize ourselves. Perhaps not at the time, but eventually, things have a way of righting themselves. So I didn't protest when Nelson said he was putting for par.

He skillfully stroked the ball, and it died just as it reached the hole. Plunk. He was home safely.

I stepped up next. There were only four feet between me and the hole, but sometimes those four little feet can seem like forty.

I wanted that par. I'd already dropped a stroke with my faulty tee shot, and I wanted to hold my score even. I pulled the clubhead back; and just as I did, I twitched. My ball slid to the left of the hole. Damn.

It was a self-penalty, I imagine, for having been willing to break the rules. Or perhaps it was a penalty for stubbornness. Either way, I deserved it.

I tapped in for bogey.

Byron Nelson's most enduring legacy is his streak. He won eleven tournaments in a row in 1945. That accomplishment was so extraordinary that now, more than fifty years later, everyone still remembers him for it. He'd lived his dream, and I figured there was a clue in that for me. I asked him about it.

He was plainspoken and modest on that subject, just as I'd expected him to be. "I'm always amazed that people think so much today of what I did so long ago," he said. He rested his golf bag to the side of the green and settled in.

I could tell he enjoyed being asked about the streak.

"I have to back up a little bit," he said, "to tell this story properly. To understand what I did in '45, you have to look at '35. I worked very hard, for a long time. There were a lot of disappointments. Times when I should have won, but one thing or another happened and I didn't. I quickly learned that golf shows the inner man. If I wasn't playing well, it was because I had an important lesson to learn. I took the more difficult road to my streak. I didn't try to get there the easy way; I just improved, slow and steady, each and every year.

"Now, golf is like life. If you resolve to learn the lesson that every situation has to teach you, you're going to learn what the good Lord put you on this earth to learn, even if it's hard.

"I can't promise you'll have a streak right away, but I can promise you'll have a streak eventually." Nelson's accent grew even thicker as he became more animated; I enjoyed hearing him pronounce *can't* as *cain't*.

"Every good golfer has lofty goals. If you want your life to count for something really special—well, you've got to aim to win, not just to be in the money. So to speak." Nelson chuckled at his own analogy.

"Do you see what I'm getting at, Zachary? To understand what I did in '45, you have to look at the groundwork I'd been laying for years."

Nelson was such a thoughtful and moral man, it made me think more deeply about my own life.

"Playing the perfect round is a symbol of something more to me, Mr. Nelson." My tone was reverent. "You inspired so many people with your streak. I want to do something like that. Not win eleven tournaments in a row," I clarified hastily, laughing. "I don't think I could do *that*. What I mean is, I want my life to count for something."

"That's what I'm trying to tell you, Zachary. You're already on the road to what you want. Remember the ten years of hard effort I put in? Well, you're right smack in the middle of your own hard work."

"I am?"

"God gives us all little missions. They're kind of like practice runs," he explained. "Little problems help you build a strong character. That way, when the time for the big mission comes, you'll be ready."

"But what am I supposed to be doing?" I asked. "You were supposed to play golf. Is it the same for me? Am I supposed to turn back the clock and try to go pro?"

"Hmmm." Nelson thought about that for a minute before responding. "You're wrong about me—about playing golf, that is. My mission was to inspire people. To show them something that'd never been done before. I guess if you want to figure out the meaning of your life, you've got to look at the foundation you're laying. What's important to you?"

"Golf. And family." I thought for a little while. "And helping others. That's why I like my job: because I get to help so many people."

"Seems to me you're a teacher of sorts, Zachary."

"A teacher?" I'd never thought of myself that way before. "What am I supposed to be teaching?"

Nelson smiled, his whole face aglow. "You've got to figure that out for yourself," he said, but I was convinced he already knew the answer.

I SPOTTED A LEADERBOARD at the seventeenth hole.

Nelson was the leader at six under. Palmer was quickly closing in with one of his famous charges at five under.

Nelson noticed me looking at the board. "Right now, I'd rather be a stroke behind Arnie than a stroke ahead of him." He chuckled softly at his own joke; but in spite of his humor, he looked a little scared, too.

I scanned farther down the leaderboard and saw my own name up there. I was the last entry on the board at four over, but I was up there nonetheless. The thrill of seeing my own name with those six legendary golfers was . . .

Wait a minute. Six? There were *eight* golfers out today. I counted them in my head. Hagen and Nelson. Palmer and Nicklaus. Player and Lema. Hogan and Jones.

That was it.

Hogan and Jones were missing.

"Where's Mr. Hogan's name?" I asked. "And Mr. Jones's?"

Nelson squinted at the leaderboard and then laughed. "Oh, that'd be Ben's little joke on us."

I drew my face into a silent question.

"He likes to keep us guessing. Probably won't turn in his scores until we finish. He did that last year, too. Got a big kick out of it. You see, Hagen teed off first, as he always does—only that time, instead of goofing around, he played to win. He led all eighteen holes and finished at six under. But Ben kept his scores a secret until the very end." Nelson laughed at the memory. "Hagen was preening over his 'victory' as Ben holed out on the eighteenth.

"'Come congratulate the new champion,' Hagen said to Ben.

"Well, Ben put on this sweet voice and said, 'Walter, thank you very much.' He shook his hand, and then showed Hagen his scorecard. Ben was *eight* under. Eight birdies and not a single bogey.

"Walter looked plumb silly, since he'd been bragging for the last half-hour about beating us all. But he played it off well. He was always one to appreciate a good joke. He and Ben settled their differences over a few drinks at the bar."

Looking at the leaderboard again, Nelson said, "If Ben wants us to know what he's shooting, he'll post his scores. If not—well, that's just Ben."

"What about Jones?" I asked.

"Bob'll keep quiet, too, out of courtesy to Ben."

I strained to look through the trees of the adjoining fairway, hoping to get a glimpse of that most famous pairing: Ben Hogan and Bobby Jones. There was no sign of either one.

8 *The Secret of Love*

When I was a little boy, I was fascinated by prisms and rainbows. I was amazed that a single crystal triangle could produce such a myriad of colors. Now my dreams of turning pro seemed to be like that old prism. I turned them right and then left, and got an entirely different picture of my life.

Perhaps Nelson was right. If I wanted to know the meaning of my life, I had to look at the foundation I'd laid. Golf, family, traveling, helping people.

The harder I thought about it, the more it seemed to me that everything in my life had been leading me to West Wind. But why?

I thought back to the beginning of my day, to the cars I'd seen in the course parking lot. The Porsche was Tony Lema's, and the late-model Cadillac—well, it had to be Ben Hogan's. Hogan's golf had a dignified gleam to it, just like the Cadillac. In fact, the more I pondered the events of the day, the more the specter of Hogan seemed to loom over me. He was the lone figure I'd seen on the driving range. He and Jones had been the first players to find me. I played with Hogan irons. The key was obviously Hogan. I knew I had to find him.

I said good-bye to Byron Nelson at the tee of the seventeenth hole, but before I left, I asked him what Hogan was really like. All the history books had called him an enigma.

"Well," Nelson replied, "Ben keeps his own counsel. I'm his friend—probably as close a friend as he ever allows—but I don't really know him. I'm not sure anyone does."

"Why the mystery?"

"The secrecy is a protective device for Ben, I think. Golf is the only thing that ever truly got into his heart."

"Do you think he'll share his secret with me, the way you've shared yours?" I was growing more and more convinced that my destiny was somehow linked with Hogan's.

"I don't know," Nelson said honestly. "As long as we've been meeting here, we've never played with anyone outside of us eight. So novelty is on your side. But then again, he *is* Ben." Nelson paused, considering the likelihood that Hogan would share his secret with me. "I don't know, Zachary. I just don't know."

Sometimes a man must go in search of his destiny. Greatness doesn't find us by happenstance; we go forward to meet it. So, with all the passion and longing I once felt for my golf scholarship, I searched for Ben Hogan. I wasn't going to let another opportunity slip away.

As the hole doglegged left, I turned right toward a pass in the evergreens. Just before I stepped into the shroud of trees, I looked back at the tee box. Nelson was alone, his figure silhouetted against the mountain backdrop. Fog hung in the valley crevice behind him, and frosted mountains rose in the distance.

The air on this mountain course was thinner and somehow purer than what I was used to. It made me think more clearly. The cobwebs were brushed from the corners of my life, and I saw my dream to play on the pro tour in a new, unfiltered light. *Things are not always the way they seem.* Perhaps my destiny hadn't been to take that golf scholarship but to entwine my life with the game of golf.

Looking at the misty, distant figure of Byron Nelson, a sureness grew within me. As Nelson had felt the stirrings of destiny in 1945, I now felt the same lure pulling me onward. I stepped across the threshold of the fairway into the silent grove of trees hoping to find the last, most elusive pairing of the day: Ben Hogan and Bobby Jones. I figured they'd be on the eleventh hole.

So far, I'd played with each other pairing. Hagen and Nelson had been first. The next grouping was Player and Lema, and then Nicklaus and Palmer. Hogan and Jones would be the last pair of the day.

Cutting through the trees, I doubled back to the eleventh box. It was empty. Looking at the tenth green, I saw that it was unoccupied as well. Should I go forward or back? I took a deep breath and decided to play forward.

As I stepped up to the eleventh tee, I felt a surge of confidence. I recognized the hole! It was an exact duplicate of the eleventh at Augusta National, the start of Amen Corner. Pines shaded the fairway, and just for a moment I could have sworn I saw dogwoods peppered throughout the woods.

The hole beckoned to me. No one really knew the best path to the cup at Augusta, just as I didn't know the right path today. We were on our own, that hole and I.

It was a long par four, the green protected by a small lake to the left. The water was a constant danger, because the green sloped toward it. The wind was a factor, too. I heard the swirl of a westerly breeze echoing down the fairway.

I pulled out my driver, and I pulled out Nicklaus's secret of attention as well. After teeing the ball, I leaned on my driver as though it were a cane and visualized the exact spot where I wanted my ball to land. I scanned the undulating fairway and chose a spot just over the second swell. I imagined my ball landing there, and then I imagined the flight pattern, backtracking my thoughts all the way from end result to beginning swing.

I was pretty pleased with myself as I fired the ball, landing it where I'd imagined I would. The secrets I'd learned today were like extra clubs in my bag, each one for a different purpose.

Looking at my second shot, I noted that it was downhill the entire way to the green. A small stream fed the lake, which billowed next to the green. Hogan, I imagined, would fade the ball in and land it well right of the water. Nicklaus would probably do the same thing.

I pulled my five-iron out of my bag. *Trust yourself.* I could hear Player's harmonic African voice whispering his secret of unity in my ear.

As I stepped up to my shot, I heard a faint whoop in the distance. I stepped away and wondered whose gallery had cried out. Was it Hogan's?

I fought the urge to run down the fairway toward the sound and stepped up again. I fired my second shot and drew it toward the flagstick, dangerously close to the water. It flew over the flag by about twenty feet, hitting the back edge of the green. It seemed to stick. But then it started rolling back toward the pin. Just one revolution at a time, it turned slowly, slowly. Then it picked up a little speed, rolling to within eight feet of the cup. A very makable birdie putt.

"Wooh!" I let out my own cheer of excitement.

The secrets I'd learned thus far weren't so much secrets to playing golf as laws of nature. Just as universal laws such as gravity influence the physical realm, so the secrets I was learning influence the realm of golf.

The green glistened in the afternoon sun. The wind had whipped it into a slick pane of grass. Stepping up to putt, I felt like one of the masters myself.

I was putting for birdie from just a hair over eight feet away. I hunched over my putt and took a deep breath. As I exhaled, I drew the putter back and stroked the ball. It went rolling toward the hole, entire minutes seeming to pass with each revolution.

Just as my ball neared the hole, it began to break. Slowly. The ball caught the outer lip of the cup, and that was just enough to knock the ball off balance and drop it in. A birdie.

"Yes!" I dropped my putter and pumped my fist in the air. I'd done it! A birdie! I could taste the sweetness.

The distant gallery cheered again, and just for a second, I wondered if they were clapping and shouting for me. As I walked to the twelfth tee box, I realized I was wrong. It wasn't a gallery; it was Arnie's army.

Instead of finding Hogan, I'd run smack into Arnold Palmer and Jack Nicklaus. Perhaps I wasn't the master of my destiny after all.

"Hey, guys," I greeted them. "We meet again."

"So we do," Palmer said coyly. "Did you have fun with Nelson?" He chuckled a little bit, implying, I thought, that Nelson's lesson of integrity was perhaps a little less than fun.

"Yes, I had a good lesson." I winked at Jack, and he winked back at me. Arnie might tease me about Nelson's lesson of character, but

I knew Nicklaus would understand just how important it was to develop inner strength.

"You guys sure are playing slowly," I said. "I've played, what . . . three holes since I left you, and you've made it through only one?" Nicklaus was a slow player, but he couldn't possibly be *that* slow.

"Arnie was signing autographs," Nicklaus said. "He signs every darn one of them."

"Hey," Palmer interjected, "I owe these people more than just good golf."

"Arnie!" someone in the ghostly gallery called out. "Sign my hat?"

"Sure." Palmer reached for it.

The man gestured at him with a pen, and Palmer drew back as if it were a lethal weapon. "Whoa. I've got a pen," he said. Quietly, he turned to me and explained, "I'll sign everything. I just don't want people shoving pens at me." He chuckled. "I ruin about 365 shirts a year from pen marks."

Palmer pulled a pen out of his own pocket and signed the hat with a flourish. He offered the hat to me.

"Me?" I questioned. "I'm nobody."

"Everyone is important," Palmer said. "Sign it."

I did. It was kind of fun, too. I brandished the pen dramatically and signed my full name: Zachary Thomas Tobias. I underlined it with a big swirl.

Palmer laughed and handed the hat back to the gallery member, who looked at my signature with more than a little dismay.

"First rule of being a golfer: sign everything you're offered. First rule of being a human being: you make a difference in this world," he said.

Palmer made me feel good, and I remembered the tiny spot of warmth in my gut when I'd first met him. That feeling grew now, spreading throughout my whole body.

"Shall we?" Palmer gestured at the tee box.

As I stepped up to place my tee, I forgot about my search for Hogan and grew eager to play with Palmer. Oftentimes in life, you go after one thing and get another. I'd gone in search of Hogan and had found Palmer. Perhaps there was something deeper at work here, a force greater than my conscious desires.

Suddenly, I remembered Nicklaus. He stood back, smiling shyly. Recalling the gallery's obvious preference for Palmer, I felt a little embarrassed at my own eagerness to play with him.

"Jack?" I motioned.

"Go ahead, Zach," Nicklaus said. "It's okay." He wasn't talking just about my having honors; he was giving me permission to bask in the reflected warmth of Arnold Palmer. "Every now and then," he said, "you should be with someone who can light up a room. Amen Corner is Arnie's favorite spot. Enjoy it. You'll learn something from him. I know I did."

I smiled again, this time warmed by Nicklaus the champion. He might not light up rooms, but the Bear brought his own style to the game.

A LEADERBOARD HUNG over the twelfth hole. Palmer had birdied eleven to jump into the lead, but Nicklaus had birdied also and was hovering dangerously behind him. Palmer glanced up at the board with naked ambition and noted his position:

| Palmer | -6 |
| Nicklaus | -5 |

Desire dampened the air like humidity. Palmer obviously wanted to win; just as obviously, he wanted to beat Nicklaus.

Looking at the two men, I noticed a strange relationship between them. They had the magnetic attraction of opposites.

Palmer was slim, while Nicklaus was chunky. Palmer was outgoing, Nicklaus was shy. Palmer had the love of the gallery, but Nicklaus had the raw talent. Strangely, when paired together, they made up a whole.

Nothing happened by chance at West Wind, and I wanted to know why Jones had paired these two men together.

"What's the connection between you and Nicklaus?" I asked Palmer. "It's almost as if you two are mirror opposites."

"What I have, Jack wants," Palmer said dryly, "and what he has, I want."

I remembered the old days of Palmer and Nicklaus duels. It had been exactly that way: each man wanting what the other had. In the early sixties, Palmer had been king of the golf course when a young Nicklaus had come on the scene to end Palmer's reign prematurely. Now, hearing Palmer's voice twinged with regret, I knew he remembered.

"Golf isn't always about what you want. Sometimes it's about what you're called to do," Palmer said. "To understand what it is between Jack and me, you have to go back to the beginning."

Palmer tapped out a cigarette and carefully went through the ritual of lighting it. He held the cigarette firmly in his mouth, struck a match, and inhaled deeply, crossing his arms as he did. He drew on the cigarette for what seemed like days, staring straight ahead, the blank focus of his eyes not on the course but on his memories. He blew the smoke out in a steady stream, and it settled over the tee box in a heavy mist.

He told me a story, a tale that began in Pennsylvania in a small kingdom named Latrobe. It was about an ordinary boy who became a king.

"I grew up in a western Pennsylvania steel town. Not a likely place for a king, is it?" he said. "How about you, Zachary?"

"Northeast Philly. Torresdale. I lived on a golf course, right behind the fifth hole."

"The fifth hole?" he questioned. "That's interesting. So did I." He took another long drag of his cigarette, and as he did, I looked carefully into the face of Arnold Palmer. Like me, he was a slender man with broad shoulders tapering to thin hips. He looked more like a middleweight fighter than a golfer. His face was heart-shaped, and a wayward tuft of blond hair fell over his forehead. Looking at Palmer, I could have been looking at myself. Our features were virtually identical.

"Living on the golf course wasn't in style when I grew up," Palmer continued. "My father was the greenskeeper at Latrobe Country Club, so we got a house near the course. Families with money lived in town."

"It was the same for me, too," I said. "My family wasn't poor, but we didn't have a lot either. Just a normal working-class family. We lived *behind* the golf course, not really *on* it. There was a fence separating my backyard from the fifth green at Torresdale."

Palmer took another drag. "I didn't have a fence to separate my house from the fifth hole at Latrobe, but there was another kind of fence all the same: between club members and nonmembers. I couldn't play the course or even play with the members' kids. Class distinctions were very clear."

I nodded, understanding perfectly how it had felt to grow up in a country-club atmosphere without really being a part of it. I'd been a caddie at Torresdale; Arnie had been the greenskeeper's son—and there was a world of difference between kids like us and the club members.

"I looked over that fence, too, Zachary," Palmer said, seeming to read my mind. "But I learned early on that anything might be accomplished if only I was bold enough to try.

"When I was about six, maybe seven years old, I had this little cut-down golf club. I used to practice whacking a golf ball. After a while, I got pretty good at it.

"Our house butted up against this one hole that had a creek fronting the green. I used to sit and wait for the lady golfers. Back then, I was just a little tow-headed kid, but I could knock the heck out of that ball. Whenever a group of ladies came up to the hole, I'd offer to drive the ball over the creek for them for a nickel." Palmer let out a throaty cigarette chuckle. "My father tanned my hide for that one, but the ladies just loved it. I earned a few nickels—but more than the money, I learned to be bold."

Palmer carefully balanced his cigarette butt between his thumb and forefinger and flicked it into the woods. "Even then, I wore my heart on my sleeve. Always did."

Palmer told me about his rise from commoner to prince. He won the 1954 U.S. Amateur and shortly thereafter turned pro. He was just one of a dozen kids turning pro and might have been lost in the crowd except for that unique Palmer quality of showing his heart.

Little boys are taught to hide their feelings. You learn, early on, that if you want to win something, you'd better hide the extent of your desire, because if you show your feelings and lose, you're going to be called a sissy.

Not Palmer. He had the muscle to back up the heart. He competed and earned the right to wear his heart on his sleeve. Palmer was the most masculine of men, deemed more manly because of his indefatigable spirit. He always tried, no matter how desperate the odds, no matter how far behind he was.

It was at the 1960 U.S. Open that he was crowned king. When Arnie told me the story, I was convinced it was his heart that had earned him the crown.

"Going into the final round, I was in fifteenth place. I was seven strokes behind the leader, five behind Ben Hogan. But I figured I had a chance." Palmer laughed. "I *always* figured I had a chance. I said to one of the sportswriters, 'I may shoot 65 out there. What'll that do?'

"'Nothing,' he said. 'You're too far back.'

"I just laughed. Nobody was going to tell me I was out of it. I said, 'Well, it would give me a 280. Doesn't 280 always win the Open?'

"Back then, the final two rounds were played back-to-back on Saturday. At precisely 1:45 P.M., I marched out to the par-four, 346-yard first hole. I hadn't been able to reach the green with my tee shot on that hole in the first three rounds. Nonetheless, I hitched up my pants, tugged at my shirt sleeves, and pulled out my driver."

Palmer chuckled. "I wasn't going to lay up, and I wasn't going to hide how I felt. I wanted to win that tournament, and I was damn well going to drive the green. I figured if I could hit it, I might just have a chance at shooting 65. And if I could shoot 65, I might just have a chance at winning the whole thing.

"On the first hole, I drove the green and two-putted for birdie."

On the second hole—another par four—Palmer sank a thirty-five-foot putt from the fringe for his second birdie. On the third, he hit his approach shot to within a foot of the hole. His third birdie. An eighteen-foot putt drained on four for a fourth consecutive birdie, and he recovered from a tee shot in the deep U.S. Open rough to save par on five.

On number six, Palmer sank a twenty-five-foot birdie putt, and on number seven he shot his approach wedge to within six feet of the hole, allowing his sixth birdie putt of the day to dart into the cup. Six birdies in seven holes.

In the dramatic, come-from-behind style that was his signature, Arnold Palmer did indeed shoot 65, and he won the U.S. Open with a 280.

"When other guys might be playing for fourth place, I was always playing to win," he said. "You might call me bold, or reckless, or even crazy, but I'm always going to play to win. I'd rather win one tournament in my life than make the cut every week."

WINNING WAS IMPORTANT to Arnold Palmer, and he wanted to win today at West Wind. Palmer took another glance at the leaderboard. He was one stroke ahead of Nicklaus. The gallery gathered like vultures on the hill behind the tee. They looked hungry for excitement.

We surveyed the short par three. A placid green was set behind a wide mountain stream. The green sloped dangerously toward the water; a pair of bunkers guarded the back edge, and another bunker fronted it.

"This particular shot," Palmer whispered, "varies between a five-iron and a nine-iron depending upon the wind. I've seen Hogan hit a six-iron to the center of the green, and I've seen Jones splash a five right behind him."

Nicklaus was oblivious to our conversation. His faded blue eyes focused on the target, one ear cocked to listen to the wind.

"One fifty-five to the green," Palmer continued.

I turned my cheek to gauge the direction of the wind. It was helping us. "A two-club breeze?" I offered.

Palmer nodded and pulled out a seven-iron.

A ripple of anticipation ran through the crowd. All eyes focused on Nicklaus, to see which club he would choose. He ran his hand over his bag, resting his fingers first on his six-iron, then on his seven.

Palmer stepped up to hit. He balanced his feet, shifting his weight from right to left and back again like a pendulum. When he was perfectly balanced, he tightened his grip and fired.

His ball shot over the green. The crowd drew an anxious breath, and we watched it slam into the back bunker.

"Ohhhh," the gallery groaned in disappointed sympathy.

Nicklaus was next. His hands still hovered over his bag. Tentatively, he pulled out a seven-iron. A twitter ran through the crowd. A seven was too much, as Palmer had just shown. The gallery grew excited at the prospect that Nicklaus, too, might falter.

Nicklaus placed his ball and gripped his club. He waggled, balancing his not-insignificant weight as he did.

He didn't swing, however. He waggled again, seemingly uncomfortable with the club. Staring at the hole, he waggled a third time and then stepped away. He resheathed his seven-iron and pulled out a six.

The gallery was abuzz. Nicklaus was going with *more* club. Nervous spectators whispered to one another. Surely this was a crack in Nicklaus's judgment. If he overshot the green—dare they hope for such a thing?—Palmer might pick up another stroke, in spite of his faulty tee shot. The crowd shifted, convinced that they were about to witness a bloody mistake.

As Nicklaus waggled his new club, I noticed something about the wind. The trees in back of the green caught the wind like a sheltering net, pushing and swirling the air around the green. The helping breeze Palmer had felt was now gusting back toward us.

Nicklaus hit a full six-iron. His ball shot toward the green, seemingly on target. The sun splashed in my eyes, and I lost sight of the ball. Someone in the gallery clapped.

I shaded my eyes and caught sight of Nicklaus's ball hitting the lower tier of the green.

"Oh, no," a voice in the gallery exclaimed suddenly. Nicklaus's ball bit the lower edge and slid backward into the semirough, toward the water.

Time stopped as I watched Nicklaus's ball slip down the precipitous slope. The rough was barely deeper than the green. Was it enough to stop the slide? The water rippled in anticipation, but mercifully the ball held, just inches above it.

The gallery hooted, eager to see Nicklaus meet with danger.

With Palmer above the green with a seven-iron, and Nicklaus below it with a six, I had no idea which club to choose.

I was thankful that the gallery ignored me. I wasn't the focus of the day; I wasn't even in contention. Sighing with relief, I ran my hand over my bag.

Sliding out a six-iron, I felt a wave of energy run through me. At first, I thought it was the wind, but then I looked over at Palmer. His army gathered around him, pulsing with admiration. I was glad they were ignoring me, because I was able to see what attracted Arnie to his army.

It was love. The force of the spectators' admiration and respect rippled toward me—first one wave, then another.

When I turned back to my ball, I flushed pleasantly and was oddly happy to know that such a love existed.

I tried to pull my thoughts back to my shot, but instead I remembered a time when I'd been walking among the sand dunes at the beach and had stumbled over a hill to find two lovers locked in an embrace. Then, too, my heart had pulsed with the unexpected discovery of love. I'd slipped away unnoticed but had carried the spark of their romance within my own heart. The spark of Arnie's army now flamed in me as well.

I gripped my six-iron confidently and decided to try for a birdie. I inhaled on my backswing, paused infinitesimally, and then let out my breath and all my strength in my downswing.

Club and ball collided, and I heard that beautiful, inimitable sound of a club being hit on its sweet spot. Before I even saw where my ball landed, I was pleased with myself.

Palmer straightened up as he heard my clubhead strike the ball, his gaze riveting on the green.

My ball plunked precisely twelve feet from the hole, just left of the pin. The water didn't threaten me, nor did the bunkers.

The gallery let out a surprise wallop of applause, and I blushed at what I'd done.

AFTER SOME DEBATE, we determined that Palmer was away. His ball was wedged under the lip of the back bunker, while Nicklaus's was on the slope fronting the green.

As we walked over the small bridge that led to the green, the gallery rushed behind us. They flooded the short fairway to line the near edge of the creekbed. Only a few feet of rippling water separated us from the craning crowd.

Palmer stepped down into the bunker to hit, and as he did, he hitched up his pants. When things were going his way, Palmer always hitched up his pants.

He was hitting two, as was Nicklaus. I knew Palmer wanted to maintain his lead on the hole. Nicklaus would most likely two-putt, so Palmer had to get up and down in two also.

Palmer tested out a few swings, trying to get the feel of the shot that would extricate his ball. He stepped up and gave the ball a whack. It hit the edge of the bunker, leaped out, and ran toward the hole.

"Ohhhh!" The crowd grew excited.

The ball slammed to a halt two feet from the cup.

"Yes!" Palmer threw his visor up in the air and bounced out of the bunker like a pogo-stick.

Nicklaus lumbered toward his ball. I could feel the pressure of a birdie in his step. If he two-putted this hole, he'd remain a stroke behind Palmer. That was unacceptable to Nicklaus.

He squinted at his ball. It looked virtually impossible to sink from where it lay on the grassy slope fronting the green.

Nicklaus bent to pick up a few pine needles that had fallen behind the ball. I saw him finger the rough as he did, apparently testing its depth. He took out his putter, and the crowd mumbled in criticism. A wedge was the more logical choice.

As he crouched over the ball, his putter looked small and impotent against the sloping rough, but he rapped the ball with confidence. It skittered up the slope, hot and fast.

I held my breath as it ran toward the cup.

The ball hit the outer edge of the cup, knocking itself off balance. Centrifugal force whirled the ball around the edge, and just when I thought it was going to ring off, it dropped in for a birdie.

The crowd exploded. Nicklaus had made a deuce and was now even with Palmer.

The king had a rival.

THE EXCITEMENT OF THE MATCH bled into my own game, and my putter got hot.

It happens to every golfer, eventually. Palmer's creed echoed in my ears: "The correct number of putts that should be taken by a good golfer is one per green."

My ball lay twelve feet from the cup, and I was putting for birdie. I stroked the ball, and it ran home.

Clunk.

My score dropped to two over for the day; I was picking up strokes as quickly as I'd dropped them, and I felt my touch would last forever.

Palmer mugged at the gallery, grabbing a white towel from his golf bag and pretending to wave it like a flag of surrender in response to Nicklaus's and my birdies. Lightfooted, he danced up to his putt, a slight two-footer.

He tapped in for par, and the crowd cheered.

I saw a different side of Palmer as we walked to the thirteenth. He was worried. He'd played a magnificent hole on twelve, but it wasn't enough to stave off Nicklaus's advance. The two were tied at six under.

Palmer would have preferred that Nicklaus rival him for the gallery's adoration, because the one thing Nicklaus threatened was the thing that meant the most to Palmer: winning the tournament. Ironically, the gallery stood behind Palmer, win or lose.

"It happened as soon as Nicklaus joined the tour in '62," Palmer said. "His star was rising and pushing mine into descent."

Palmer paused to light another cigarette, leaning against his golf bag as he did. "I had an inkling of what was going to happen. I remember the first time I met Jack. It was in 1956 at an exhibition match in Ohio. We had a driving contest, and I beat him by a bit. After that, I kept an eye on him and was aware of what he was doing in golf. You never know how someone's game will develop, but with Jack I figured it was just a matter of time."

I heard a twinge of sadness in his voice. As Palmer had been at the top of his game, winning tournaments and charming the galleries, he'd kept watch over the rising star of a young Ohio golfer, sensing that his own time as a champion might be cut short.

"I was the favorite for the '62 U.S. Open," Palmer said, taking a long drag of his cigarette. "I'd already won my third Masters in April, and the Open was going to be held thirty-five miles from Latrobe at the Oakmont Country Club, a course I'd played maybe a hundred times.

"I wanted to win. Oh, yes," he laughed ruefully, "I wanted to win more than anything." He thumped his cigarette ash off.

With 72,000 people in the galleries, the '62 Open at Oakmont shattered all previous attendance records. It was as if the fans knew something special was building. Prophetically, Palmer and Nicklaus were paired together for the first two rounds, Nicklaus the tour rookie and Palmer the Masters champion. The pairing set the tone for everything that was to follow in the lives of these two great men.

On the final day, Palmer holed out with a total score of 283. In the eyes of Arnie's army, love had swept the hometown hero to victory, for in the three previous U.S. Opens played at Oakmont, only Ben Hogan and Sam Snead had broken 290.

But Nicklaus outdid Palmer on the final day with a sub-par round and came from behind to match Palmer's 283, tying for first place.

"There was an eighteen-hole playoff on Sunday," Palmer recounted, his eyes misty with the memory. "I remembered what I'd said about Jack—that we'd all better watch out for him—and it haunted me."

Arnie's army was in full battle dress that day. When Palmer teed up his ball, they cheered. They stampeded from tee to green, convinced that the power of their support would sway the match in Palmer's favor.

After eight holes, though, Nicklaus was ahead by four strokes.

"I knew I had to make something happen," Palmer said. "I figured the ball was just sitting there. Nobody had stepped on it or was trying to keep me from hitting it. I just went ahead and did the best I could."

Palmer birdied the ninth. And the eleventh. And the twelfth, to close Nicklaus's lead to one.

"But then I faltered," Palmer said, the pain still fresh in his voice. "I bogeyed thirteen, and Jack's lead was two again. It stayed that way until the final hole. Jack was just so damn good. The better I played, the better he played."

Arnie's army formed a brigade of faith around the eighteenth green. The rough was deep, and the fairway was narrow on that long par four. A birdie from Palmer and a bogey from Nicklaus would push the tournament into sudden death. The gallery hoped—no, they *knew*—Arnie could do it.

"Jack hooked his tee shot into the rough," Palmer said. "Mine landed safely in the fairway."

The army cheered in support.

Nicklaus slashed at the rough but couldn't reach the green. In fact, he still had nearly a hundred yards to go, and he was lying two.

Palmer pulled out a long iron and fired at the pin. His army pulsed with all the love they could muster, but it wasn't quite enough. His ball landed short.

Nicklaus took aim, and his third shot landed twelve feet to the left of the cup.

Palmer was hitting three. He pitched at the hole, and his ball seemed to fly directly at it. For a fraction of a second, his army thought they'd been victorious. If Arnie could hole this shot, he'd get his birdie.

Palmer didn't hole out, though. His ball rolled ten feet past the hole.

"Nicklaus was putting for par," Palmer said. "I never gave up, not even on those final strokes. If Nicklaus three-putted and I holed out, we'd be tied."

The heavyset golfer crouched over his putt, the pressure of Arnie's army pulsing in his ears. He stroked the ball, and it rolled two feet past the hole.

The gallery cheered as Palmer stepped up to his ball.

"As I stood over my ball," Palmer said, "I remember thinking that if I holed out and Nicklaus missed again, we'd go into sudden death. That's where I made my mistake—thinking about something besides hitting the ball."

Palmer stroked his putt and missed. Nicklaus holed out and became the 1962 U.S. Open champion, his rookie year on tour.

"In ninety holes of golf, I'd three-putted only once," Palmer said. "I was proud of how I played at Oakmont, and that's what made my loss all the more heartbreaking. Now I knew that even if I played my best, Nicklaus might still beat me. When the Open was over, I told everyone, 'The big guy is out of the cage; everybody better run for cover.'"

Palmer thumped his cigarette and was quiet. He stood with his hands clasped against his throat, chin resting upon them. The pain of his '62 Open loss weighed heavily upon him. He didn't say a single word against Nicklaus, but I knew his hurt ran deep. He'd been the king of golf, beloved by all and feared by his competitors, and then—literally, in a single day—Nicklaus had come along and stolen his crown.

NICKLAUS PLAYED OUT HIS MAGIC on the thirteenth hole at West Wind, forgoing the love of the gallery for the pleasure of winning. Palmer continued to play with his heart, but it was painful to watch him struggle.

We stepped up to the thirteenth tee box, and Nicklaus readied his drive while Palmer hung back, quietly regarding the hole. His loss of honors was an extra burden on his slim figure.

The thirteenth at West Wind completed the loop of Amen Corner. It was a short par five, easily reachable in two if it weren't for a small creek that ran down the left border of the fairway and curled in front of the green, ready to catch any shot that was slightly off line.

Nicklaus set his drive to draw around the left corner, and he pounded it safely into position.

As I stepped up to hit, I glanced over at the gallery. The spectators were looking at Palmer with naked admiration. He might have parred the last hole, but in their eyes he was and always would be the king. As I had on the last hole, I felt the pulse of their love surround me, and I drew energy from them.

I hit an intentional hook that flew safely around the dogleg and out of sight. I felt sure it landed in a good position.

Palmer was last. He swaggered to the tee, his doubts tucked away, and was on the attack once again. He smashed an enormous drive, and when we rounded the corner, we saw that it had landed a good twenty yards beyond Nicklaus's.

There was only one problem. I couldn't find my ball.

"Not again," I whined. My drive had cleared the left-hand grove of trees; I knew it had. The fairway, though, was punctuated by only two white balls: Nicklaus's and Palmer's. There was no rough along the left border, which left only one possibility: the creekbed.

With growing dread, I walked toward the creek and peered into the water. Nothing.

I tilted up my visor and rubbed my forehead in confusion. Where the hell was my ball? It just wasn't possible that I'd lost *another* ball on this course. Not two in one day; the golfing gods couldn't possibly be so cruel.

"Hey, Zachary," Palmer shouted. "Look at that!" He pointed across the creek. There was a bank of flowering bushes and a small strip of rough grass fronting the far side of the creek.

And there was my ball, sunk amongst the rough, safely landed on the wrong side of the creek. I laughed.

"If you can find it, you can hit it," Palmer said. "If you can hit it, you can probably move it; and if you can move it, you might as well be able to knock it in the hole."

I continued laughing at his logic, supposing that he was, technically, correct.

Wading across the creekbed, I found my ball tightly banked in the rear by the bushes. I wasn't able to take a full swing, and I wondered how far I'd be able to advance the ball. Probably only twenty or thirty yards. I'd be safer to just pop the ball over the creek, land it in the fairway, and get it on the green in three. Hagen would've been proud of me; I didn't let my detour bother me a bit.

Grabbing my seven-iron, I punched the ball out.

THE GALLERY LINED THE RIGHT EDGE of the fairway, and they mumbled opinions as Nicklaus stepped up to his approach shot.

The key decision was whether to lay up or go for the green. The creek curled dangerously around the green, ready to punish the slightest inaccuracy. The pin was tucked in the left front portion of the green, making the gamble even more enticing. Laying up could possibly net a birdie, as could going for the green.

Nicklaus pulled out his seven-iron; he was laying up. The crowd buzzed, taking Nicklaus's choice as a sign of weakness.

Nicklaus ignored the gallery and lobbed his shot to the end of the fairway for two. He now had just a short wedge over the creek and a likely one-putt for birdie—and a one-shot lead if Palmer made par.

Palmer's drive had been longer than Nicklaus's. He stepped up to it and regarded the hole solemnly. Was he going to lay up, or go for the green?

The gallery chirped with excitement.

With his signature gesture, Palmer hitched up his pants and pulled out his four-iron. He was going for the green. Someone in the gallery clapped, and my heart leaped in anticipation. We all knew that, in the end, Palmer would go for the green, but somehow watching him decide heightened the drama.

His desire for a birdie carried to me like a scent on the wind.

Palmer slashed the ball home. It flew straight at the water.

"Nooo," the gallery moaned.

Palmer's ball seemed to hit in slow motion. I saw it drop into the creek; I saw the splash of water; but then, miraculously, the ball deflected off a rock and bounced out. It ran for the green, skipping thirty feet past the pin.

"Yessss," the crowd cheered.

Palmer threw his iron in the air in amazement.

Nicklaus and I could do nothing but shake our heads.

As I stood over my third shot, I glanced at Arnie's army. I liked playing in front of them. They were wild in their devotion to Palmer, stampeding down the fairway to get a glimpse of him, groaning and roaring all the time. It was marvelous fun. They made me feel as if I were part of something important, something exciting, and I felt their enthusiasm work into me like a spiritual amphetamine.

I was hitting three, with nearly two hundred yards to the green, and all I could think of was, *Go for it.*

Grabbing my two-iron, I addressed the ball and took a mighty swing. My ball flew at the pin, straight over the creek, and spun to a halt on the back tier of the green.

The gallery roared in approval.

Nicklaus, Palmer, and I marched down the fairway. Palmer was lying two on the green, thirty feet past the cup. Nicklaus was lying two, just a pitch away from the cup on this side of the creek. Both men were tied at six under.

Nicklaus continued to stalk Palmer. He surveyed his ball like prey, circling it, testing the wind, judging the lie. He pulled out his wedge and, with the dexterity of a master craftsman, nipped the ball across.

The gallery hooted in dismay as Nicklaus's ball ran up to the hole, directly on line. It bumped across the green, just one dribble, then two, and slid into the hole.

The crowd was stunned. Nicklaus had knocked it home for an eagle.

"Yes!" Nicklaus pumped the silent air. As Palmer drew energy from the army that adored him, Nicklaus seemed to draw skill from their disapproval.

Palmer stood there, stunned. He'd thought a birdie would be good enough, but with that one stroke, Nicklaus had pulled ahead.

"I'd better make something happen, hadn't I?" Palmer said to the astonished gallery.

"You can do it, Arnie!" they shouted in response.

Palmer leaned on the gallery's enthusiasm, and I noticed a lightness in his step as we crossed over to the green.

Palmer was hitting three, with a slippery thirty-foot putt home.

He crouched over his putt, pigeon-toed and knock-kneed. He carried the same putter he'd used in high school. It was scarred and scratched from use, but still lethal.

The gallery jostled for position, pushing and straining to get a glimpse of their hero.

Palmer was bothered by the movement. He stepped back and waited, moving forward again only when the crowd was calm.

He quietly read the line and steadied himself. He wanted this eagle putt, wanted to match Nicklaus stroke for stroke and maintain his own dominance over the game.

Again, the gallery jockeyed for position.

Palmer's nerves were taut. The movement of the gallery prompted him to step back a second time. He took a deep breath, then came back and took his position. Nothing twitched in Arnold Palmer. He hunched over his putt and stroked the ball.

It began rolling toward the cup. Palmer's fate seemed to hang on each revolution of the ball. If he sank this putt, he'd stay even with Nicklaus and perhaps slow the onslaught of this new young talent.

In the end, Palmer left the ball short. The gallery cheered, but Palmer's shoulders slumped in disappointment.

He tapped in for birdie and realized, once again, that no matter how well he played, Nicklaus was always going to play just a little bit better.

It seemed cruel to me that Jones had paired Palmer and Nicklaus together. Nicklaus had to deal with a brutal, taunting crowd, and Palmer had to relive the pain of losing. My heart broke for both of them.

Awash in sympathy, I stepped up to my own birdie putt. I felt an inner connection with Nicklaus and Palmer, as if I alone had seen behind their public faces into the heart of their game.

Strangely, this knowledge resonated within me and flowed into my putter. I rapped my putt, and it skittered to the hole, holding its line.

My heart rose in my throat as I realized it was going in.

"Yes!" Palmer, Nicklaus, and I shouted at the same time.

It was my third birdie in a row.

"WHATEVER ARNIE WANTS, Jack gets," Palmer said quietly. "That's how *Time* magazine summed it up."

"But you didn't stop winning," I said hopefully.

"Oh, no," he continued. "I won two more majors after Jack joined the tour, but it wasn't the same. After my loss at the '62 U.S. Open, I knew my time had come to an end, and it was hard for me to take."

The next year, in 1963, Nicklaus won the Masters, Palmer's favorite major. Palmer was never in contention. As the defending champion, he helped Nicklaus don his first green jacket, an irony not lost on the crowd.

"Winning was everything to me," he said. "I didn't play golf to place in the money or even to win regular tour events. I played to win majors. To me, that's what really defines a champion—how he can hold up in the majors.

"The old magic came back to me from time to time, just to remind me of what I'd lost. At the '66 U.S. Open, at the turn of the final round, I was ahead by seven strokes. Nine holes to go and a seven-stroke lead." He shook his head in regret. "I still can't believe what happened. My lead bled away, and I finished in a tie with Billy Casper. It's funny, but at the turn Billy looked to me and said, 'I'm going to have to really go just to get second.'

"I reassured him, saying, 'Don't worry, Bill: you'll finish second.'"

It was ironic that Palmer was the one comforting his competitor, filling Casper with the confidence that would lead to his eventual victory. *Or was it?*

A sly smile broke across Palmer's face. "It's very important to me that the good guys win at the end of a movie."

But how had this movie ended? Palmer won the '62 British Open and the '64 Masters, his last major victory. He won seventeen more individual tour events, but in 1973—at the age of forty-four, when most golfers are hitting the peak of their careers—Palmer stopped winning. His victories trickled down, fewer every year, until finally he stopped winning altogether.

Both he and Nicklaus bore scars from their duels. Nicklaus had gone on to win more major titles than any other golfer in history, but the gallery's early open hostility had hurt him. Palmer, too, remembered the sixties with pain. How many majors might he have won had Nicklaus not come on tour? More than he cared to count.

"There's something I don't understand," I said. "You stopped winning, and Nicklaus never really won the gallery over the way you did. Who's the winner?"

Palmer looked up and flashed his photogenic smile at me. His whole body seemed to radiate, and once again I was warmed by his personality.

"We both did," he said.

I raised my brows in silent question.

"Winning was everything to me. As I told you on the last hole, I always felt that I'd rather win one tournament in my life than make the cut every week. For Jack, it was important that the galleries like him."

"So neither of you got what you really wanted."

"On the contrary, Zachary. We both got what was truly important. There are times in your life when you go searching for something, but instead of finding what you're looking for, you find something else of greater value."

"You went after winning. What did you find instead?"

"Love," Palmer said simply. "I found something more valuable to me than all the tournament victories in the world. I found the love of the fans, and it's never deserted me, even when my golf game left me."

"But it seems that Nicklaus got the better end of the bargain," I said. Why did Nicklaus settle for winning when Palmer settled for love? Wasn't it possible to have both?

"Nicklaus got the trophies," I continued, "while you had to settle for the fans. Does that mean love is more important than winning? That you're better than Jack?"

"Each person has his own destiny, a particular—and important—meaning to his life. When you put it all together, you have a whole."

I considered those words for a moment. Palmer and Nicklaus did seem to fit together, mirror opposites of the same destiny.

"My life had one purpose, and Jack's had another," Palmer continued. "I wanted to keep on winning more than anything; I didn't want to give up being the king. But when you submit to the higher purpose for your life, you find your destiny.

"If you could just dream up goals and use spiritual principles to go after them, life would become meaningless. There'd be no adventure." Palmer smiled broadly. He liked adventure.

"Life isn't about what you choose but about what you're meant to do. Jack was meant to put aside his desire to be loved and reach his potential to win tournaments. I was meant to do something different."

"You were meant to love," I said softly.

"Yes," he agreed, nodding. "When you begin to discover your purpose on earth, you find the force that created you. That force is love."

GOLF WOULDN'T HAVE BEEN as exciting without either Jack Nicklaus or Arnold Palmer. This, I think, is why Jones, in his dry cosmic wit, had paired them together. They were one. Within the history of their competition, I saw the seeds of destiny they'd planted for me to discover.

Golf showed me the depth of my heart. I'd gone in search of the perfect round but had discovered something more important en route: love.

Love had drawn me into the game. It was the energy that sustained me. The undeniable sound of a golf club being struck on its sweet spot, the soar of the ball rising toward its target, the beauty of the course surrounding my every step—these were the things that pulsed through my golfer's heart.

And so, like Arnold Palmer, I followed the love.

9   *The Secret of Fearlessness*

almer had turned the prism to yet another angle, and I saw that everything had led me to this one moment in time. Life wasn't about golf scholarships or playing the perfect round. Life was about doing what I was meant to do. There was one single reason I was on the course today, and I finally understood what it was. I was there to help Hogan win.

Think about it. I felt destined to help others, and Hogan was beginning to be a recurring theme in my life. So how could I help Hogan? By helping him win. That's what Hogan wanted most in his life: to win.

I bade good-bye to Palmer and Nicklaus at the fourteenth hole, leaving them to finish their perpetual duel the way it had always been, the way it would always be.

"You sure you want to look for Hogan?" Palmer had asked me before I left.

"Yes." I was positive. "He's supposed to win, and I'm supposed to help him." I tilted my visor up to rub my forehead. "When I met Hogan this morning on the first hole, he looked right through me. Scared me, too. He seemed to see all my faults. But you know something?"

Palmer leaned on his golf bag and looked interested.

"Hogan limped a little when he walked away," I continued. "Not that most people would've noticed. It was just a slight shuffle. But it struck me that for all his mechanical precision, Ben Hogan is very human."

"You know the limp is from his accident," Palmer remarked.

"Yes. The accident."

In 1949, when Hogan was at the peak of his golf game, the car he was driving was hit head-on by a Greyhound bus. Hogan's legs had been crushed; the doctors had said he'd never walk again, much less play golf.

"Be careful, Zachary," Palmer said. "Hogan can be mighty prickly when someone cuts into his privacy. He doesn't like to talk much."

"Oh, don't worry," I assured him, laughing. "Hogan'll love me."

"I played with Hogan once. In 1960. I was my usual self."

"Hit it, go find it, hit it again?"

"Yep." Palmer laughed. "Hogan made a textbook par three on the first hole. My first shot landed in a tree stump, my second hit the edge of the green, and I holed a forty-foot putt to match his par. On the second hole, Hogan split the fairway, ran one onto the green, and two-putted for a classic par four. I drove into three inches of water, squirted it out onto the fairway, slammed my third shot beyond the green, and chipped in for par. Finally, after two more holes of this, Hogan turned to me with those gunmetal eyes and said"—here Palmer lowered his voice for his best Hogan imitation—"'Look, damn it; we're here to play golf. Stop fooling around.'

"He scared the bejesus out of me," Palmer said soberly.

PALMER AND NICKLAUS TRUDGED OFF, and I situated myself across from the leaderboard. Hogan and Jones had to come along some-time; they were the last pairing of the day. No use stressing myself out running all over the course, lugging my golf bag. I'd wait for them to come to me.

So I laid down my bag and stretched out on the ground beside it, cradling my head in my arms. The leaderboard showed every player except Hogan and Jones and what they had scored on each hole. I was anxious to learn how the other masters had been doing while I was playing. Although I couldn't see any of the players, I could picture the action by following their scores on the leader-board.

I noticed that Walter Hagen had carded a villainous triple bogey on twelve. Ouch. Those strokes really cost him. He spent the next several holes desperately searching for a birdie but coming up dry. While Nelson and I had been on number fifteen, Tony Lema held steady on thirteen to sink his seventh consecutive par of the day, and his playing partner, Gary Player, broke his own string of pars to birdie and jump to four under. At this point in the round, Byron Nelson was in the lead, but four hungry golfers were staring him down.

Nelson	-6	15		Lema	-4	13
Palmer	-5	10		Hagen	+2	16
Nicklaus	-4	10		Tobias	+3	15
Player	-4	13				

A twig dropped out of the trees behind me and plunked on my shoulder, startling me. I looked down to brush it away. When I turned back to the leaderboard, I was surprised to see fresh scores posted.

I still don't understand how the board got updated so frequently. Perhaps it was in one of the alternative realities Bobby Jones had told me about. All I know is that every time I looked away—even for a fraction of a second—new scores were posted. I have to admit, though, it was a convenient system.

Taking a closer look at the board, I saw that Hogan's scores were posted. This was, perhaps, a bigger shock than the self-updating leaderboard. Nelson had told me that Hogan rarely posted his scores, preferring to play his own game. From what I understood about Hogan, his every move had meaning. Ben Hogan did nothing by chance. Why the deviation now?

Hogan and Jones were on number eight. Hogan had just finished a run of birdie, par, birdie; he stood at three under. Jones was steady with Old Man Par.

Player and Lema were on fifteen. Lema had pulled his tee shot on fourteen out of bounds and ended with a double bogey, and his mistake bled over into his game on fifteen where he bogeyed, dropping to one under (and out of competition). Player responded to his own bogey on fourteen differently. He steeled himself—and perhaps took a nip of raisins—to birdie fifteen and recapture his position at four under. Player was in the hunt, two shots off Nelson, but he was running out of holes.

While Player was struggling to regain his unity, Nicklaus, Palmer, and I had been on thirteen, the final turn of Amen Corner. I remembered how Nicklaus had had a magnificent run of birdie, birdie, eagle. Now I saw those holes within the context of the whole match—Nicklaus had leapfrogged over Nelson to take sole possession of the lead at eight under. Palmer, unable to match

Nicklaus, had finished our play at thirteen with a disappointing bird, one stroke back at seven under.

Hogan and Jones seemed to be playing in an insular world, unaffected by the shuffling on the final holes. Hogan nailed his third consecutive birdie on ten to advance to five under, while Jones made his first birdie of the day on nine and then a par on ten to stay respectably behind the field at one under. Ever the gentleman, Jones rose above the fracas.

The leaderboard was crowded underneath Nicklaus, any one of three golfers within striking distance:

Nicklaus	-8	13	Jones	-1	10
Palmer	-7	13	Lema	-1	15
Nelson	-6	17	Hagan	E	18
Hogan	-5	10	Tobias	+1	13
Player	-4	15			

Nelson and Hagen were the first to hole out. Hagen carded an even par 72, while Nelson bogeyed the final hole to finish at 67. Nelson had posted the final score to beat: five under.

Player was on seventeen. He'd parred sixteen and had only two holes left to make something happen. Drawing from the well of indomitability that had won him nine major championships, Player eagled seventeen to better Nelson by one stroke.

I was practically glued to the leaderboard by now, watching the match develop simply by following the scores.

Nicklaus and Palmer imploded. The run of perfection stopped for Nicklaus as he bogeyed two holes in a row, dropping to six under. Nicklaus's bad golf bled onto Palmer, and Arnie pulled his tee shot into the scrub brush and had to take a lost-ball penalty for a wicked double bogey. He bogeyed again at fifteen and dropped to four under, going the wrong way on the leaderboard.

Meanwhile, Hogan and Jones were on twelve, just two holes away from me. Hogan was at the turn of Amen Corner and had just sunk his second consecutive par. He'd avoided the water on twelve, but he was still one stroke back at five under.

I wanted Hogan to make something happen. Birdie. Eagle. Going for the green. *Anything.* Thus far, he'd played a flawless round. Five birdies and not a single bogey. All he needed was one or two more birds to win.

Hogan was playing Amen Corner conservatively, but Jones thrived on the challenge with a bird on eleven and a deuce on twelve. He hopped up the leaderboard to three under, a polite two-stroke distance behind Hogan.

Nicklaus	-6	15		Jones	-3	12
Player	-6	17		Hagen	E	final
Hogan	-5	12		Lema	+1	17
Nelson	-5	final		Tobias	+1	13
Palmer	-4	15				

Hogan was now one hole away on thirteen. Any minute now, I'd see his familiar hawk profile scanning the fourteenth hole, with me by his side.

I noted the new changes on the leaderboard. Player and Lema had holed out. Lema's slide continued with a bogey, bogey, par finish. He carded out at 73, presumably joining Hagen at the bar. Player holed out with a birdie to take sole possession of the lead at seven under.

Damn. Another stroke for Hogan to make up.

Nicklaus and Palmer were on sixteen now, where Nicklaus parred to stay at six under and Palmer bogeyed again to slide to three under. They had only two holes left to play—not much room.

Hogan's scores on thirteen were posted. He'd sunk his third consecutive par. He must have laid up on thirteen, taking three strokes to the green and a two-putt for par. Damn it, Hogan, I silently cursed. Pick up the pace. You needed a birdie, not a par.

There were only five holes to go and Hogan was two back. The closer Hogan got, the more I wanted him to win. I had a feeling that if he could win today, it would mean something important to my own life.

Jones birdied thirteen, threatening Hogan at four under. Jones's own run of three consecutive birdies seemed to be a message to Hogan rather than an exercise in golf perfection.

CRRRACK. BEHIND ME, I heard the sweetest sound in golf—the sound of a club being hit precisely on its sweet spot.

Crrrack. There it was again.

I scrambled to my feet, and as I turned around, I saw Ben Hogan and Bobby Jones walk onto the fourteenth tee.

Crrrack. Incredibly, Hogan echoed his golf when he walked. His steps sounded exactly like his swing. I'd long since ceased to be amazed by the mystical happenings on this course, so it seemed perfectly natural for the rifle-crack sound of golf to herald Hogan's arrival.

Crrrack. The course let loose one last, sharp sound, and Hogan stood in front of me. He stared at me from beneath his trademark white-linen cap, and I grew a little nervous.

"Mr. Hogan," I said deferentially. I could think of Palmer as Arnie, but Hogan would always be *Mister* Hogan.

He responded with a curt, almost dismissive nod.

Jones turned to me, his voice liquid with welcome, as if to make up for Hogan's abruptness. "Zachary," he drawled, "I'm glad to see you again. Have you been enjoying your day?"

"Oh, yes," I said, and the details of my play spilled out of me. I told Jones about my glorious birdies and my vicious triple bogey, remarked on the importance of the lessons I'd learned, and mentioned how much I'd looked forward to playing with him and Hogan. "I'm so grateful to you both for letting me join you today. For letting me"—I stumbled over my words as I glanced at Hogan—"for letting me join you now."

Jones put a warm hand on my shoulder, apparently understanding the allure Hogan had for me, and gently nudged me toward his friend. I tried to say something intelligent to draw Hogan out, to prove I was worthy of helping him, but the best I could do was begin with a stutter: "Um, Mr. Hogan? I see you're two strokes back from the lead. I, um, I really hope you win. No, that's not what I mean. I *know* you'll win. It's just . . . important . . . that . . . you . . ."

Hogan's stare burned, and I looked away, suitably chastised. But then, in a gentlemanly gesture as unexpected as his slight limp, Hogan softened: in a quiet voice—no louder than a murmur, really—he said, "I believe Bob has honors." There was to be no preamble, no conversation, just a continuation of play. Then again, Hogan *was* going to let me play with him, and he wasn't barking at me. I figured I'd scored a point or two and stood back to let Jones hit.

The fourteenth was a short par four. It had nearly unassailable defenses. Tall, stately pines lined the fairway, lending a delicious feeling of seclusion to our play—the way Hogan preferred it, I imagined. A drive was out of the question. There were two bushy pines that pinched in the fairway some seventy yards from the green. A large arrow-shaped bunker lurked a bit closer to the tee on the left side of the fairway, ready to catch a timid shot. Precision, not power, was the essence of this hole.

Jones teed his ball. The sunlight darted through the pines and cascaded over him, bathing him in an aura of pure white. As Jones stood over his bag, selecting his club, he continued to glow. I wondered if Hogan noticed, or if it was only I who saw Jones's purity.

Jones played with the clubs of the twenties—a spoon instead of a three-wood, a niblick instead of a seven-iron. He named his clubs, too. His driver was Jeannie Deans; I saw her battle-scarred head peeking out from the top of his bag. Calamity Jane, the putter I'd swung with my own two hands, was there, too.

Spoon in hand, Jones let loose a swing of slumberous grace. With all the smoothness of a sweet iced tea, Jones swept the ball safely onto the landing area.

"Ben?" he invited, gesturing toward the tee box.

Hogan was smoking as he stepped up to the box. He pinched his cigarette, sucking the very life from it, and stared down the fairway. His face was a mask. He wasn't picturing his ball sailing toward the perfect spot, as Nicklaus had done—of that much I was certain—but I couldn't discern what Hogan *was* thinking. He pitched his cigarette to the side of the tee, as if something important had been decided, and took out his three-wood.

Crrrack. Hogan lashed into the ball with blinding speed. The sound of his club's impact was the most perfect and pure sound I'd ever heard and probably ever will hear. That sound belonged only to Hogan.

As soon as he'd swung, Hogan turned his back to the ball, sleeving his club in his bag. Apparently, he'd felt the perfection and knew, before the ball ever hit the ground, where it would land. But I *had* to watch; I couldn't turn from the relentless flight of Hogan's ball.

It landed just shy of the guarding pine trees, a good pitch up to the green. The ball impacted and spun slightly to the right, perfectly on line with the clearing to the green. I'd seen magnificent golf played today, but nothing compared with this shot.

Jones cleared his throat, stirring me out of my reverie, and I placed my own ball. Hogan seemed to examine my grip and stance, and it made me nervous. I swung, slamming my ball right into the fairway bunker.

"I don't know why he wants to play with me," Hogan said to Jones. "He should be practicing." He picked up his bag and started down the fairway. I had to hurry to catch up with him.

Hogan needed to make something happen if he intended to win this game. Wanting him to exert his magic, I hovered over his ball like a moth seeking nourishment from a wool sweater.

I wasn't worried about myself. I'd blasted my ball from the bunker into the safe landing area just shy of the evergreens. A pitch and a putt and I'd make par. Jones's second shot, a niblick, had landed on the green, and he was also in line for a par. But Hogan needed a birdie. He was two strokes back with only five holes to play. A par wasn't good enough.

"Are you aiming for the pin?" I asked. "You know, one of your nice fades would spin the ball into position for a birdie putt." I thought a little advice might help.

Hogan sliced through me, and my suggestion, with one look.

Yikes. I took a step back to get out of his line.

Hogan was ninety yards off the green, a large heart-shaped affair with a deep guarding bunker. Nothing was rushed about Hogan. He quietly regarded the green, tested the wind, and unsheathed his pitching wedge. With great deliberateness, he hit his ball to the right of the pin. Crrrack. The only thing he did fast was swing. His ball bit and spun left, leaving him a twenty-foot birdie putt.

My fears about Hogan's position doubled. His putting—once precise before the accident—was now infamously inept. I didn't want to admit it, but I doubted his ability to sink a birdie putt of that distance. Once again, my purpose at West Wind crystallized in my mind: I was here to help Hogan win. And he obviously needed me.

Knowing how prickly Hogan could be, I offered my advice as gently as I could. "You can pick up a stroke on the next hole," I said, with an eye toward boosting his confidence. "It's another par four, but Player birdied it; and if he can, you can, too."

Hogan said nothing.

"What I mean is," I explained, "it's okay if you par here. The greens are really slick, and it's okay if you two-putt."

Hogan looked at Jones and said, "Is he going to play, or stand here talking all day?"

Hmpf. Hogan wasn't making this easy on me. I cast him an irritated glance and bumped my third shot up on the green, to the left of the pin. When we got to the green, however, I immediately understood why Hogan had hit his shot right—and why my advice had been, perhaps, a bit premature. There was a dangerous swale to the left, and my ball sat precariously in the middle of it. I might have only fifteen feet to the pin, but Hogan's twenty-foot putt was infinitely easier, a straight line.

We putted out in silence.

My putter stayed hot, despite the difficulty, and I rapped in for par; Jones two-putted to match my score. When Hogan stepped up to putt, his body was perfectly still, but his pants legs were shaking. Again, I got a glimpse of the private Hogan, the man who could precisely fire an iron-shot to the correct plane of the green but who was scared by a twenty-foot putt.

He rapped the ball with a perfectly tuned *thwack* and sent it sliding to the hole. It ran on line, and my heart pounded as it neared the hole.

Closer. And closer still. It ran true and then—just as it neared the threshold of the cup—stopped. It was less than six inches short.

Hogan tapped in for another par, his fourth in a row.

I'D LIED WHEN I TOLD HOGAN that he could birdie the fifteenth. It was the site of my own triple bogey, and I knew it was a treacherous hole to play. Only Player had scored three here today. Nelson had parred, but Lema, Nicklaus, and Palmer had all bogeyed. If Hogan bogeyed also, he'd drop three behind the lead, a deficit he surely wouldn't be able to overcome.

I didn't know what to do for him. My talking irritated him, as did my meager attempts to bolster his confidence. There seemed to be a definite reason Hogan did everything, so I had to assume he knew what he was doing.

But he was making me very nervous. I didn't want my mission to fail.

Jones still had honors. He drew Jeannie Deans from her scabbard and hit an enormous drive, one I would have thought impossible for a 1920s driver. Perhaps Jones's drowsy swing had hypnotized the ball into doing his bidding. Whatever the reason, the drive mounted the long rise of fairway to reach a narrow landing area.

Hogan stood back, silent as ever, waiting for me to hit.

I declined, explaining that I'd already played this hole, and the next, with Nelson. Frankly, I had no desire to repeat my triple-bogey performance. Furthermore, I didn't think Nelson would approve of my playing the hole twice. My score was my score, and I'd just have to be honest about it.

Hogan regarded the hole with his customary thoroughness. He lit a cigarette and seemed to draw half of it into his lungs with one long drag. Again, I wondered what Hogan was thinking about. He seemed to have a purpose to each shot, but I couldn't figure out what it was. In my opinion, he needed a birdie, but he seemed to be playing for par.

Crrrack. Hogan let loose a perfect drive. It landed, incredibly, twenty yards beyond Jones's. All *right!* Now he was getting somewhere, playing the way I thought Ben Hogan should play.

As soon as Hogan hit his shot, he started walking down the fairway—a cold, determined stride. He left his golf bag sitting beside me and Jones.

"I think he means for you to caddie for him," Jones said.

I didn't care too much for Hogan's manners, but maybe if I were his caddie, he'd start talking to me and tell me how to help him. I got pretty excited at the prospect. With Hogan's shot making and my desire for him to win, how could we be anything but an unbeatable combination? I slung his bag and mine over opposite shoulders and lumbered after Hogan.

I took my new job as his caddie seriously. Hogan had been playing much too conservatively. With me at his side, this tournament was his to win.

We waited as Jones hit his second shot to the green. He swept a beautiful two-iron, but the green was slippery and his ball slid forty feet beyond the pin.

Walking the twenty yards to Hogan's waiting ball, I carefully dusted off his clubs and recommended a two-iron.

"Give me the three," he said softly.

"But you can get to the pin with a two-iron and set yourself up for a birdie putt," I protested.

"Give me the three," he repeated.

"But—"

"Zachary," he interrupted. "Shut up and give me the three."

I did as I was told. As I'd feared, Hogan spun his second shot too far from the pin for a birdie. I was going to have to nip this in the bud. Hogan needed to be playing for birds, not for pars.

I started out delicately. "You know, Mr. Hogan, twelve and thirteen were good birdie opportunities. Since you played conservatively there, we need to make something happen here. You've got to start playing aggressively."

Hogan didn't say anything.

"You must have laid up on thirteen," I continued. "Now, I'm not questioning why you did that—"

"Zachary." Hogan almost spit the word out. "I'm a five-time U.S. Open champion, I can show you the medallions to prove it, and I'm getting tired of your damn advice. Shut up and carry my bag. I didn't need a birdie on thirteen, and I don't need a birdie on this hole."

Didn't need a birdie? He was two strokes back with only four holes to go, and he didn't need a birdie?

"And quit rattling the clubs," he barked, taking off ahead of me.

I STOOD QUIETLY ON THE EDGE of the green. I'd pulled the flagstick and handed Hogan his putter, and now I was waiting for him and Jones to hole out.

Why on earth would Hogan say he didn't need a birdie?

Either he didn't want to win . . . No, I quickly dismissed that option. The Hogan I'd read about pursued excellence with relentless determination. He'd rejected the doctors' prognosis after his accident and had walked and played championship golf again. He'd never settled for second place when first was within his reach. I concluded he must have a plan.

At the 1950 U.S. Open at Merion, his first major tournament after the accident, Hogan had played and won with absolute perfection. He'd played the entire four rounds without a seven-iron in his bag. When the reporters had asked him about that, he'd replied, "There isn't a seven-iron shot at Merion."

Hogan was a field marshal. He made a plan and stuck to it, always expecting himself to be able to replicate his shots time after time, whether under tournament pressure or in practice. If Hogan said he didn't need a birdie on thirteen, or now on fifteen, then he must have a plan I didn't understand.

However, the prospect that Hogan would play conservatively on birdieable holes simply because he already had his birdies planned was frightening. Was Hogan so precise, so perfect, that he could produce birdies on the final holes of a round to come from behind to win?

Thwack. Hogan's perfectly aimed second putt broke my train of thought, and I saw him hole out for par. Jones did the same. We walked to the sixteenth. Hogan was still behind by two, and my own desire to see him win increased in pitch.

The sixteenth was a long par three. I whispered to Hogan, "One-ninety-one to the green."

He nodded, pulled out his three-iron, and stood back for Jones to hit.

I never tired of watching Jones swing. It was the loveliest sight in the world, a perfect pendulum. From my caddie's perch behind the tee box, I watched Jones's ball fly toward the hole, reach the center crown, and dribble over the upper plane to the hole. Jones was in line for a birdie.

Crrrack. Hogan was quick. He shot the ball with a piercing trajectory and landed it right next to Jones's, a short ten feet from the cup. Apparently, Hogan had marked sixteen as a birdie hole.

As I lumbered toward the green, Hogan's bag over my right shoulder and my own over my left, I noticed something different about the course.

There was no gallery now. No sign of the ghostly faces that had lined the grassy avenue when I'd played with Nicklaus and Palmer, no trace of the crowds' ever having been there. West Wind gave each player the conditions he desired, and from the silence of the course, I determined that Ben Hogan most loved the solitude of golf.

The wind rustled the trees, as if to hush even my thoughts.

I tried to work out the mystery of the Hogan enigma while we walked down the fairway, trying to discover new ways to reach the man. I laid out the other masters' comments about him like shiny pebbles in a row:

Byron Nelson: "Ben never liked being around a lot of people. I don't think anyone ever realized how shy Ben is. It's not that he's cold; he just can't talk to folks while he's playing. It's what he has to do to concentrate."

Tony Lema: "Ben Hogan is the best shot maker there ever was. He can make a plan and stick to it under enormous pressure."

Bobby Jones: "Without a doubt, Ben is the hardest worker I've ever seen. Not just in golf, but in any sport. His recovery from his accident was no less than I expected of such a champion."

Gary Player: "Ben Hogan is absolutely fearless."

Hogan's spirit was made not of light but of steel. He formulated a plan, refused to be distracted, and went after his goals with the same rifle-crack hardness he employed in his shot making. Not even a Greyhound bus traveling at forty-five miles an hour could deter Hogan.

As we stood at the edge of the green, I tried to coax Hogan's secret from him. Maybe eliciting *his* help was the way to reach him. "I really want you to win today," I said. "I know it means something significant to my own life, but I don't know—"

Hogan interrupted me with a grunt, but helping him was so important to me that I risked continuing. "Why is playing with you so significant to my life?" I asked.

"What do I look like, the answer-man?"

My adrenaline was flowing now, and I pleaded with him. "But

all the other guys told me their secrets, and how they applied to me. Can't you just—"

"I had to dig my answers out of the ground. Dig yours out yourself." His tone was sharp. "Nobody ever helped me." Hogan paused to light a cigarette and then continued in an uncharacteristic torrent of words. "You think you can just come on a golf course and have dead people tell you all the secrets to life? We worked hard to get here, and we worked hard for our secrets. What kind of cushy life do you have?"

I turned to Jones, hoping he'd intervene. He did, but not in the way I thought he would. Instead of support, I got more confrontation.

"Destiny isn't a neat little package, Zachary," Jones said. "You've come to us today to meet your own destiny, the way each of us eight met ours. It isn't something that can be dictated. It comes to you in bits and pieces. Ben's right. You have to figure it out for yourself."

Dejectedly, I handed Hogan his putter. I didn't think either he or Jones was being fair. Everyone else had been so clear about his secret. Why was Hogan so enigmatic?

Jones stroked his putt in for a birdie, and then Hogan took his stance. I tried not to care, but my heart raced as I saw Hogan crouch over the ball, his pants legs shaking once again.

He had only ten feet to go. If he made it, he'd close the gap between him and Player to one stroke.

Hogan tapped the ball lightly. The greens were like ice, and his ball seemed to slide to the hole. It died just as it reached the cup, teetered on the rim, and then dropped in.

Clunk. A birdie.

HOGAN STARTED WATCHING ME.

I know he didn't want me to see him doing it, but I did. I was very quiet. I wiped his putter clean, sheathed it in his bag, and took off for the seventeenth tee box, careful to wrap a towel around his clubs so they wouldn't rattle.

I knew I'd be playing the seventeenth, my second-to-last hole of the day, but I didn't give Hogan's bag back to him. His legs had to be tired, and I was still young, so I continued to carry it.

If Hogan could be fearless, so could I. Perhaps, if I followed his example, I'd learn why it was so important to me that he win. I'd been suitably chastised by both him and Bobby Jones, so I set out to map my own inner landscape rather than relying on the masters to do it for me.

A leaderboard was posted at the seventeenth. Nicklaus and Palmer had holed out, leaving only Hogan, Jones, and me on the course. Nicklaus had birdied seventeen but bogeyed eighteen to end his round at six under, one stroke back from Gary Player. Palmer had rallied for a birdie, birdie finish, but that still left him two strokes behind Player at five under 67.

Hogan was tied with Nicklaus for second place. If he could snatch two more birdies from this course, he'd win outright. One birdie would give him a tie and push him into a sudden-death playoff.

I took a good look at the seventeenth and began to map out a birdie for myself. Perhaps Hogan's secret for me lay in emulating him: making a plan and sticking with it. As I counted my shots, I was embarrassed to realize I was talking out loud. "Tee shot to carry the fairway bunker. I can make it if I pound my drive. Second shot, long iron to the green. Two-putt for birdie."

Hogan shuffled behind me.

"Mr. Hogan," I said. "Are you ready for your driver?" I hustled to his bag and pulled off the head cover.

"My legs are tired." His voice was soft as lambswool, and for the first time today, he looked not directly at me but at the ground. If I hadn't known better, I'd have thought he was nervous.

Jones backed off the tee, calling to us as he left, "I'm going to stretch my legs a bit. You two have a good talk."

I wondered if I was in trouble.

Just then, I saw a small padded bench that had been installed to the right of the teebox. Hogan sat down, and cautiously I sat next to him.

Hogan pulled up his pants legs and began to knead his calves. Both lower legs were bandaged up to the knees and beyond. I suspected that the bandages traveled the entire length of his legs, from ankle to thigh. They were heavy and elastic, compressing his legs in an effort to massage his circulation into its proper flow.

"Ever since the accident, I get tired on the last few holes," he offered.

Why was Hogan talking to me now? Had I finally done something to help him? Hogan's voice was weary, and he stumbled over his words. I considered what Nelson had said about Hogan's being shy, and so I kept quiet. I didn't want to make Hogan any more uncomfortable than he already was.

"I struggled for a very long time," Hogan said, still kneading his battered legs. "Young people nowadays don't know the meaning of struggle. That's all I was trying to say. I didn't mean to be rude. I just . . ." His voice trailed off.

I nodded in understanding. Hogan's concentration was too intense to be interrupted with my questions. I understood that now. Hogan continued looking at the ground, making both of us anxious.

"I . . . I remember a tournament," he said. "It was in 1931 in Shreveport, Louisiana. I wasn't a very good golfer back then. I didn't have natural talent like some people. Whatever luck I had, I made."

I was hypnotized in the presence of the private, human Ben Hogan. He was a shy man, nervous about talking to me—perhaps more nervous than I was. He stumbled over his words, not because he didn't know what to say but because his mind was so finely tuned that he had a hard time slowing it down to match my own, more mortal speed.

He continued. "I had to try three times to make it on tour. No one would believe it about me now, but back then, at that tournament in Shreveport, I had to sell my watch to pay my caddie." I winced at the thought of the great Ben Hogan selling his watch to pay a five-dollar caddie fee.

"I know what it's like to go down to your last dollar in pursuit of a dream. I knew tough things, and I can handle tough things. When my wife, Valerie, and I were newly married, I went on tour for another try. I didn't do too well." He shook his head with the memories, pain and pride strangely mixed together. "At one point, right before a tournament in Oakland, California, Val said to me, 'Ben, do you know how much money we have?'

"I said, 'Yes. I know.'

"She waited a minute and then said, 'Eighty-six dollars.'

"I knew she was scared, and I was, too, but there comes a time when you have to stand firm. I said, 'Val, we had an agreement to spend fourteen hundred dollars. We have eighty-six dollars left. We're going to Oakland.'

"I didn't win at Oakland," he admitted, his voice trembling slightly. "But I did place second, and I won three hundred and eighty dollars. That was the biggest check I'd ever won, and probably the most important check I ever won, too." Tears glistened in Hogan's eyes, and in mine also, as I regarded the man who'd won thousands of dollars, who was now a multimillionaire from his club manufacturing, and yet who'd gone down to his last eighty-six dollars in pursuit of a dream.

"Do you understand what I'm telling you?" Hogan asked quietly.

I nodded, and I thought I did. Hogan was a mass of contradictions. He could be brutally silent and yet infinitely tender. He was a cold and aloof man, yet one who was visibly moved by the memories of his own struggles. Ben Hogan, I realized, had a well of spiritual strength and wisdom within him that very few could comprehend.

"Stand firm," Hogan said softly. "When it gets rough, remember to stand firm."

I THINK HOGAN KNEW WHY it was important to me that he win, but he wasn't going to tell me. That was okay, because for the first time that day, I understood one of the reasons I was there.

I wasn't at West Wind to learn how to play better golf; I was there to learn how to deal with—and triumph over—what life gave to me. Life is one long round of golf, and in the middle of the round, there's no one to help you. You must do your own thinking. There are no teammates to bail you out, no coach to tell you how to make a play, no one to rely on but yourself. I knew there would come a time when I'd have to emulate Hogan, to be absolutely fearless.

I thought about Hogan's accident. His legs had been crushed, but he'd refused to give up. Golf, to Hogan, was the greatest love affair of his life. Nothing was going to stand between him and the course. Hogan's first tournament after his accident was the Los Angeles Open in 1950. No one expected Ben to finish, much less win. He played well the first day, better the second. Then, in the third and fourth rounds, he had to play through driving rain, the cold dampness paining his already tortured legs. But Ben Hogan never gave up. He tied Sam Snead for first place, and then he lost the eighteen-hole playoff by four strokes. At the champion's dinner, the famous golf writer Grantland Rice said, "His legs were simply not strong enough to carry his heart around."

Tears clouded my vision of the seventeenth fairway. I knew my time with Hogan would have great meaning in my life, if only I could stand up to life's hazards as he had.

Hogan came from behind me and put a warm hand on my shoulder, looking out at the fairway to a distance only he saw.

10 *The Secret of Destiny*

L ike a bridge to the present, the tears I shed at the seventeenth tee box that day are now in my daughter's eyes as she realizes the importance of Hogan's victory. If Hogan won at West Wind, it would be a signal to anyone who was sick, injured, or broken in body that he or she could win, too.

As I hold one of her small hands between my own rough and callused ones, I remember the wide-eyed curiosity of her youth, when I regaled her with bedtime stories of Ben Hogan's fabled victories and, like Aesop, moralized that Hogan's greatness lurks within us all.

I'd tried my best, then, to win her over to Hogan's side, but her favorite golf stories were always tales of Bobby Jones. Now she reminds me of the little girl she once was as she whispers, "Tell me about Bobby."

I don't want to tell her about Jones, because I fear what that will mean. I don't want to tell her what I learned. I don't want to face our destiny. She's insistent, however, as she always has been, and repeats, "Tell me about Bobby."

I try to swallow the lump in my throat and paint her a picture of the mythic Bobby Jones as he appeared to me on the seventeenth tee of West Wind.

Bobby Jones wore a shamrock on his watch chain. He'd been born on St. Patrick's Day, 1902. He pulled his watch from a tiny slotted pocket in his plus fours and checked the time.

"Four o'clock," he said. "We're a little early today."

"Do we have to be in by a certain time?" I asked, wondering aloud whether the magic of the day might disappear with the stroke of Jones's watch.

"Oh, no," he said, smiling. "We're all quite real."

Time was passing, however. There were only two holes left to play, and I could feel the match coming to a close. Dusk comes early to the mountains, and by four o'clock the sky was dark, crowded with clouds.

Jones was a handsome man. His mink-brown hair was carefully parted in the middle, and every now and then he brushed a wayward lock from his forehead. Like his swing, his face was soft and languid. When he smiled, the gleam seemed to start at his eyes. They twinkled with a knowing far beyond his years. Then his grin slowly stretched to the crinkly corners of his eyelids, then to his cheeks, finally dawning across his lips to light his whole face.

I felt a wet drop on my forehead. I brushed it away and looked up. Storm clouds had begun to gather. Another drop fell, then a third, and quickly a fourth.

"We'd better find cover," Jones said as the rain began to pelt us.

We scurried into the adjoining woods, finding shelter under a large evergreen. It provided a convenient umbrella, keeping us fairly dry. Every now and then, a few drops broke through the leafy covering, but I didn't mind.

Hogan lowered himself under the tree with a great deal of difficulty. He wasn't used to sitting on the ground, and his legs were too stiff from the accident to allow him to bend completely at the knees. With an awkward, jerky movement, he finally collapsed on a bed of pine needles and began massaging his legs. He seemed to be in his own world, leaving Jones and me to talk freely.

"The rain is a bad break for Mr. Hogan," I said to Jones.

"Hmmm. It would appear so," he said cryptically.

"What I mean is," I fumbled, trying to explain myself, "he's already tired, and the rain isn't helping. Do you think he'll be able to finish?"

"Ben'll finish."

I wasn't sure Jones understood what I was getting at. Hogan might *finish*, but with what score? I wanted Hogan to win; I *needed* him to win. "Mr. Hogan needs to birdie these last two holes."

"Or he could par and eagle," Jones offered. "Or *I* could win. I'm only two shots back of the lead myself."

"Are you . . ." I hesitated, incredulity audible in my voice. "Are you *trying* to win?"

"You sound surprised, Zachary." Jones laughed. "After all, I've won a few tournaments in my life. Whoever is meant to win this tournament will win it."

"What do you mean by 'meant to win'?" I asked. My voice was tentative. "Do you mean—?" Fear constricted my throat. Was Jones saying that everything in life was predestined? That I had no real control? That life was scripted, so trying to discover the meaning behind it was utterly irrelevant?

Jones interrupted me. "Zachary, there's a grander plan to the universe than we're able to see when we're alive."

The tone of his voice calmed me somewhat, and for a second I knew that Jones wasn't here on earth with me but resided in a place where beauty and harmony, not chaos, reigned. His face had a peaceful, otherworldly look.

"I don't understand." It was the only response I could make.

"I know you don't, son." Jones looked at me with a slight mist in his eyes. Of all human traits, it was the innocence of mankind that he seemed most touched by. *I* would have called my reaction ignorance, but Jones didn't. He saw the honest seeking of my heart.

"There's something you do better than anyone else in the universe."

"There is?" I was surprised. I'd always thought of myself as flawed, as someone who'd made many wrong choices and mistakes. "If I have a destiny," I ventured, "what is it?"

Jones laughed, with a twinkle in his eye that signaled an outburst of love. "It's the theme you've been drawn to throughout your life. Take a good look. You'll see that each of your experiences in life has added to the development of your special talent."

"Really?" I wanted to know more.

"Oh, yes," he said. "We're all here for a reason."

At that moment, a question about Jones's destiny popped into my head. Every golfer in the world has wanted to know why Jones quit playing tournament golf after winning his Grand Slam. When he was alive, Jones never explained. I thought he might tell me if I asked.

"Is that why you quit playing golf? Because of your destiny?"

"Yes, Zachary," Jones said quietly. "It was because of my destiny."

PERHAPS HERBERT WARREN WIND, that famous golf writer, described Jones best when he said, "Just as there was a touch of poetry to his golf, so there was always a certain, definite magic about the man himself."

"Tell me about 1930," I urged. It was the year Bobby Jones won all four majors: the U.S. Amateur, the U.S. Open, and their British counterparts. O. B. Keeler, the renowned Atlanta journalist (and mentor to Jones) who dubbed these majors the Impregnable Quadrilateral, said it was a feat never to be equaled in golf, an outcome determined by the gods.

"O. B. Keeler was the first to call my career predestined. And he was right. Before I started a match, I always knew how it would end."

"The way I know Hogan will win today, you mean?"

"Not exactly." Jones's eyes sparkled with wisdom. He seemed to understand the universe so much more than ordinary mortals. As he explained his thoughts, the rain melted around us, giving the evergreen tree the feeling of a priest's confessional.

"You see, Zachary, you're worried about the outcome of this match."

I nodded in agreement.

"That's not destiny," he said. "When destiny is in play, the outcome isn't in question.

"In 1930, the U.S. Open was held at Interlachen, in Hopkins, Minnesota," he said. "Destiny smoothed her hand across my brow during the second round, on the par-five ninth hole. I was shooting for the green, and in the middle of my backswing, I was distracted by two young girls running across the fairway. I half-topped the shot and sent it running toward a pond that fronted the green. My ball skipped—it literally skipped—across the water and landed on the green side of the lake."

"What happened?" I asked in astonishment.

"I pitched it up and sank my putt for a birdie four."

"That's not what I meant," I said, laughing. "How did your ball skip across the pond?"

"The reporters said I hit a lily pad."

"Did you?"

"No," Jones replied.

He was silent for a moment. To me, he was both priest and parishioner, a wise teacher who understood the great spiritual truths of life and also a common man like me. I held my breath, waiting for him to continue.

"Destiny," he began, "is a question your life answers. It's not something you decide but something you discover within. That's why we're drawn to the game of golf. It shows us what's inside."

The rain diminished into a delicate mist.

"Perhaps it will help you if I explain my own destiny," he said. That was the story I wanted to hear.

"In 1930," he began, "I didn't understand the reason I was drawn to win all four majors. I just knew that I had to try. The signs were all there, but it took years for the complete picture to emerge, so I acted on intuition and signed up for the U.S. Amateur, the U.S. Open, the British Amateur, and the British Open.

"You'll need a bit of history to understand. You see, Zachary, I never made a nickel from tournament golf. I started my career as an amateur, and I finished as an amateur. Even at the height of my play, I was never more than a weekend golfer. There were months on end when I never touched a golf club."

"So the stories about you not having to practice are true?" I asked.

"Well, true enough." He laughed. "But the real story of my destiny lies in the evolution of my little golf tournament. After winning all four majors, I knew I was at the end of my journey. Every time I played tournament golf, my body rebelled. I couldn't eat, I lost weight, my hands shook, and I sweated with nervousness. More than anything else in the world, I wanted to play golf for the pure joy it gave me. Not for trophies, not for glory, just for fun.

"So I built a golf course and invited some of my friends to play with me. It was the start of the Augusta Invitational, the Masters

Championship, the most revered of all the majors. It's the only tournament played for love, not money. And because of it, golf is the last major sport to retain traditional values of sportsmanship.

"That was an important part of my destiny. To keep love alive in golf. I couldn't have done it without winning the Grand Slam."

THE RAIN STOPPED, but it left mist curling over the fairway in slow eddies.

Just as Jones had in 1930, I now felt the hand of destiny wipe my brow as the three of us—Hogan, Jones, and I—crept out from underneath our sheltering evergreen and ventured back to the tee box to finish the tournament.

The seventeenth hole was a long par five, dotted with pot bunkers. Straight ahead, at just the distance of a perfectly placed second shot, was a deep, scarred trap. It looked like Hell Bunker from the fourteenth hole at St. Andrews, in Scotland. In fact, the longer I looked at this hole, the more it seemed to resemble the Old Course, and I said as much.

"Yes," Jones confirmed softly, "'tis St. Andrews all over again." His voice was reverent. "This hole and the next are identical in every regard to that grand and ancient course."

I remembered that Bobby Jones had been infatuated with the Old Course at St. Andrews, and the course with him. It was the site of his 1926 Walker Cup victory, his 1927 British Open triumph, and his 1930 British Amateur victory. Jones was forever linked to St. Andrews, so it seemed inevitable that the finishing holes of West Wind would resemble his beloved Old Course.

Jones was one stroke behind Hogan, and Hogan stood one stroke behind Gary Player, the leader at seven under. The day had come down to this final pairing and these final two holes.

Jones had honors. He wielded his driver, Jeannie Deans, as an ancient warrior might unsheathe his sword, sweeping his ball with drowsy precision just beyond the cluster of bunkers known at St. Andrews as the Beardies to find sanctuary in a soft, grassy landing field. He was safely in the fairway.

Hogan hobbled a bit as he approached the tee. His legs were stiff and tight, and again, I began to doubt his ability to manufacture the birdie we needed.

Hogan teed his ball and took a painful stance, wincing slightly as he balanced his weight.

Crrrack. His swing was blindingly fast. There was barely time for a waggle before Hogan fired his drive, landing his ball in the dangerous left rough. It was the first fairway I'd seen Hogan miss all day. The rain had been a costly turn of fate.

I gulped back my growing fear that Hogan would lose and fired my own drive into the rough.

"Hand me a wedge," Hogan said briskly as we walked off the tee. I'd grabbed Hogan's bag along with my own. Hogan needed all of his strength just to negotiate the course. A few extra pounds of iron and wood wouldn't hurt me, but for Hogan it might mean the difference between failure and triumph.

I slipped Hogan's driver into his bag, careful to clean it before replacing the head cover, and handed him a sand wedge. He used it as a cane as we walked.

The rain had slowed the course, and our drives carried for no more than 250 yards. Instead of watching our balls tumble and run, we saw them sink into the verdant carpet. Hogan and I were left with nearly 300 yards to the green.

I hit first, a solid three-wood that skirted the left edge of the fairway, fortunately shy of Hell Bunker.

Hogan surveyed the hole with absolute precision. He lit a cigarette and held it with his lips. Wispy tendrils of smoke curled about his face. His problem was obvious. Could Hell Bunker be carried?

And then quickly, his decision made, he pitched his cigarette and stepped up to the ball. Crrrack.

My heart soared as his ball took flight. Hogan's gait might have been wobbly, but never his shot. His ball landed safely beyond the danger, a nice pitch away from the green.

"Well done," Jones said as we trudged to the grassy hollow where his own ball lay. If Hogan's shot put pressure on Jones to match him, I couldn't tell. Jones's grip was steady and his swing effortless as he fired at the green.

Jones landed his ball just beyond Hogan's, safely in line for a quiet pitch and one-putt for birdie. What Hogan had done, Jones had bettered.

I had a testy third shot. The green was a shelf that tilted away from us, with the pin cut dead right. I was approaching it from the left, hardly an ideal position. Glancing at Hogan, I remembered his fearlessness. Despite the rain, despite his battered legs, he trudged on. As his caddie, I could do no less.

I quelled my anxiety and fired at the pin.

"Look at that!" Hogan's voice pierced the mist, and my head snapped up to see what I'd done. If Hogan spoke during a round, something important had happened.

My ball hit the center of the green, ran for the pin, and slammed to a halt twenty feet shy.

I picked up our bags, slung one over each shoulder, and tried to contain my excitement.

Hogan was hitting three. He had a hundred-yard pitch to the green. Using a right-hand mound as a slingshot, Hogan bumped his ball up, ran it to the edge of the mound, and then let gravity take over. It catapulted toward the cup, leaving him with a ten-foot birdie putt.

Hogan's shot had been right off the drawing board, and I slammed his wedge into the bag with an appreciative whomp. No one could touch Hogan now. One little birdie putt and he'd be tied for the lead.

I grinned wildly, utterly convinced that I was home free.

As Jones stepped up to his third shot, he asked, "Have I ever told you about my final round at Royal Lytham and St. Anne's?" Jones had a dry sense of humor. He was always slowing us down with a humorous story, an anecdote about his days in competitive golf, or an off-color joke.

Hogan and I shook our heads.

"Well, then," he said solemnly, "perhaps I should." He stepped away from the ball, tucking his club underneath his arm. "It was the 1926 British Open. The British didn't approve of playing golf on Sundays, so the final two rounds were played back-to-back on Saturday. After the third round, I was two shots from the lead.

"Ben," he said, "you understand how it feels in the midst of a major, between the third and fourth rounds, when everyone is jostling you and bothering you and begging for autographs and interviews."

Hogan nodded shyly. "For me, that was always the hardest part of golf," he admitted.

"For me as well, my friend," Jones said. "Well, at Royal Lytham, I figured I could sneak into the village between rounds and eat my lunch in peace while everyone else was in the clubhouse. I slipped away and had an enjoyable hour's break.

"I came back the same way I'd left: through the tournament's front gate. When I reentered, the gatekeeper asked to see my ticket. I showed him my competitor's badge, but that wasn't good enough. I had to buy a ticket in order to get back in." Jones chuckled. "Good thing I had a few pounds on me, because I won the Open later that afternoon."

Jones's twinkling laugh rained down upon us as he stepped up to his chip shot. He was both confident and modest, standing there with his niblick in hand, at once in control of the ball and humbled by it. The echo of his laughter still reverberated as Jones swung his hickory-shafted club.

He froze at his follow-through, club swept over his shoulder, entranced by his ball's flight. The ball hit the upper edge of the green and tumbled toward the pin.

It ran true, and I felt little pangs of fright the closer it got to the cup.

Jones's ball ran home, and I realized that if it went in, he'd eagle and tie Hogan for the lead.

The ball began to slow. I held my breath, desperately hoping that Hogan's lead would be protected. The cup was now only five feet away, and Jones's ball was rolling so slowly I could see its dimples.

The ball died as it reached the hole. Just when I thought it would stop one or two revolutions shy, it fell into the cup. Jones now held the lead with Player, at seven under.

HOGAN WAS STUNNED by Jones's eagle. His face registered surprise, then shock, then a trace of what I thought was fear. But then, almost as quickly as emotion had appeared, Hogan tucked his feelings away, visibly straightened, and became the Hawk once more, his face inscrutable.

"You're away," Hogan said softly, and I stepped up to my birdie putt. Ever since I'd played with Arnold Palmer, my putter had been hot, and it didn't fail me now. I sank my twenty-footer, a long rambling putt that seemed drawn to the cup like magnetized steel.

With six birdies through seventeen holes, I was undoubtedly playing the best golf of my life. I'd recaptured all my lost strokes and was now looking Old Man Par dead in the eye. Somewhere along the line, though, I'd lost the desire to play for my own gratification. I wanted Hogan to win; he'd become my Grand Slam. Just as Bobby Jones knew that he had to win all four majors to fulfill his destiny, so I knew that Hogan had to win to fulfill mine.

Hogan hunched over his putt. It was essential that he sink this bird.

He stroked the ball, and it ran straight for the hole, rolling along an invisible line drawn by his imagination.

Clunk. It dropped in, and Hogan had his birdie. His face was expressionless as he, Jones, and I walked to the eighteenth tee.

The tournament would be decided on this final hole. It was a replica of the eighteenth at St. Andrews, 354 yards long, a par four. Both Hogan and Jones had been beloved in Scotland, but only Jones had played St. Andrews. Was it a sign?

At St. Andrews, this final hole was named the Tom Morris hole, after the first British Open winner and the legendary father of Scottish golf. Old Tom, as he was nicknamed, took part in every British Open championship from 1860 until 1896. He would have loved Bobby Jones—of that I was sure. Jones had a style that was almost British in flavor, with his self-deprecating smile and impeccable manners.

"This is what golf is all about," Jones said as he placed his ball. "We turn the final page to see what the course has to offer us."

Jones stood over his ball and swung with his customary drowsy grace. As he watched his ball's flight, however, I caught a flash of displeasure in his eyes.

Jones had met with trouble. His ball tumbled deep into the right-hand rough. He shook his head ruefully as Hogan took his stance. In spite of myself, my heart leaped. With Jones in the rough, Hogan had an advantage.

Crrrack. Hogan was like a marksman. He fired at the fairway and hit it dead center. There was no bounce. The course grabbed and held the ball like a greedy infant.

When I reached for my driver, I could feel the blood pounding in my ears. My knees were weak, but somehow, in spite of the pressure (or perhaps because of it), I was able to hammer my drive just shy of Hogan's.

HOGAN AND JONES STOOD over their second shots discussing strategy.

"Do you think a pitch from the Valley of Sin is still safe?" Jones asked, referring to the grassy hollow in front of the green.

"When it's dry, it's perfect for a bump and run," Hogan replied.

"But the rain has slowed the course down."

"Hmmm," responded Hogan as he considered his friend's reasoning. "I think it's best to avoid the Valley altogether. Run it up from the side."

Jones nodded in agreement.

Quite frankly, I was a bit surprised to see the two men sharing opinions on this final hole. Apparently, it didn't occur to either one of them not to want the other to play well.

Jones hit first. He pitched it over the Valley of Sin, carving his shot with backspin and loft instead of the traditional low topspin.

His ball hit the green.

My heart thumped in my throat. For one brief, infernal moment, Jones's ball looked destined for the hole. But then, despite the backspin, the ball failed to stop. It ran twenty feet past the pin.

Jones was tied for the lead, on the green in two, with a makable birdie putt.

HOGAN WAS STEADY as he stepped up to his own second shot.

Crrrack. I took comfort in the familiar rifle-crack of Hogan's shot. His ball traced Jones's trajectory and lofted toward the green. It seemed suspended in flight, my heart along with it, with the danger of the Valley of Sin just below and the promise of the green just ahead.

Then Hogan's ball began its descent.

The Valley beckoned. If Hogan's shot wasn't long enough to land on the green, he'd lose the tournament. There was no way he could recover from that grass trap in time to match Jones.

His ball hit the upper edge of the green.

My sight was blurry from tension, and for just a moment I imagined that Hogan's ball slid backward into the Valley. I blinked and looked again.

This time I saw his ball sliding toward the hole and then past it. It finally stopped twenty-five feet beyond the pin.

Hogan was safely on the green in two.

THE PRESSURE WAS CHOKING ME, and I lost all sense of touch.

I felt as if I were wearing mittens; I couldn't get a feel for the club or the ball. My legs were leaden, and I heard the rush of blood in my ears, pulsing a queer, off-beat rhythm.

I slammed my second shot onto the green. My swing wasn't graceful like Jones's or powerful like Hogan's; it was a swing of pure desperation.

My ball ran up and through the Valley of Sin, barely deterred by the wet grass, bumped up onto the edge of the green, and slid down toward the pin. It finally stopped five feet short. I'd made the most effective pitch of us all—and certainly the ugliest.

Hogan was away.

He was putting for birdie, and I was praying. In the early fifties, when Hogan was capturing his most famous victories, his putting was notoriously bad. The accident had robbed him of his putting touch as well as his stamina.

Hogan's pants legs shook again as he stood over the ball. If he sank this one, he would better Gary Player by a stroke and stand in sole possession of the lead. It would be up to Jones to tie him.

Uncharacteristically, Hogan stepped away from the putt. He wiped his palms on his pants, circled the hole once again to reread the green, and stepped back to his ball. I held my breath as Hogan stroked it.

His ball ran true, closing the distance. Twenty feet away, now fifteen.

The rain had left a misty coating on the green, and Hogan's ball etched a line in the grass as it rolled.

Ten feet away, now five. Still the ball held its line.

Two feet away, and it broke to the right infinitesimally.

It slowed and then stopped.

One foot short.

Hogan's shoulders slumped almost imperceptibly. If it hadn't been for that slight droop, I wouldn't have known he was disappointed. His face was blank—expressionless as always—as he tapped in for par and a tie with Player. He walked to the side of the green to wait for Jones to putt. Somehow Hogan's slumped shoulders scared me more than his missed putt. They told me that Hogan hadn't played this hole as he'd planned.

Jones had a fifteen-footer for birdie. Calamity Jane in hand, he quietly read the green, making note of the small right-hand break Hogan had experienced.

He stepped up to the ball and swept it cleanly toward the hole. It was over in a fraction of a second. Jones's ball darted to the hole, dying just as it reached the cup (as Jones's putts always did), and fell in for birdie.

I stood dumbfounded on the side of the green.

Jones had won. He'd holed out at eight under, and Hogan had tied Player at seven. I kept going over the shots in my mind, wishing that I could find something to make it all turn out differently. A forgotten penalty, a miscount. Something. Anything.

Jones prompted me to hit, but I couldn't move. I couldn't believe I'd failed again. First my golf scholarship, then all those years of bad golf, and now Hogan.

"Zachary?" Jones prompted, and finally I stepped up to my own birdie putt and holed it to finish the round at one under. It was a strange anticlimax. I'd hit the first, and now the last, stroke of the day.

The other golfers gathered in the clubhouse, rowdily calling to Hogan and Jones. Tears clouded my eyes for a reason I didn't understand. I didn't want to leave the green, so I just stood there. Hogan put a warm hand on my shoulder and said, "Good round." He walked to the clubhouse to join the others.

Jones stayed with me.

The laughter and rejoicing of the other players faded behind us. I leaned down, pulled my ball from the cup, and slid it into my pocket. Jones turned away from the green and walked back toward the eighteenth fairway. I followed. After a bit, Jones reached into his own pocket and pulled out his golf ball.

He handed it to me.

It was the ball that had won the tournament. I fingered it softly. It was warm from the heat of Jones's body.

For a long time, neither one of us spoke. Jones knew I was disappointed, and he knew enough to leave me alone with my sadness. Every now and then his brow creased in thought, and he rubbed his chin absentmindedly as though he were sorting out a complicated puzzle in his mind. It was a puzzle that would take me twenty years to decipher.

Epilogue

Jones's golf ball is in my daughter's hand, where it's been all night. It warms me as I close my fingers around hers.

She was surprised when I gave it to her yesterday. "Oh, Daddy," she said. "It's a symbol of West Wind." I'd hoped she'd see Jones's ball as a talisman of West Wind's magic and not of my failure. It was all I had left to give her, and I hoped it would be enough.

It's morning now. Sometime during the night, I cracked a window, hoping to blow away the stale hospital smell of ammonia. Now the room is cool, and I rise to close the window.

She awakens with a sharp breath, and her eyes blink open. "Daddy," she says, startled. "You look terrible."

I do look a fright. I'm unshaven, my eyes red and bleary, my shoulders knotted and slumped from a night of worry and sleeplessness. "I was telling you stories," I explain.

"I remember. About Bobby Jones." She smiles.

"Is that *all* you remember?" I ask worriedly. "Don't you recall what I told you later? After Jones's story?"

Her eyes narrow suspiciously, and she asks, "What have you been up to?"

I run a tired hand through my hair, pushing my thinning locks from my forehead. "I told you stories all night," I say, "about Hogan."

"About Hogan?" she repeats.

"Yes. Stories about his career. Don't you remember? I told you about the 1951 U.S. Open, how Hogan studied the Oakland Hills golf course for weeks. How he analyzed every shot, pulled all his strength together, and won with a final-round 68.

"I told you about the 1967 Masters, and how Hogan, at age fifty-five, turned the magic on again, just to show everyone it was still there. Don't you remember?" My voice was growing anxious. "In the third round, he went out in 36, but on the tenth tee, he became the Hogan of old. He birdied eleven, twelve, and thirteen."

Tears pour from my eyes once again. She *has* to remember. She has to forget that Hogan at West Wind. She has to remember that he walked away from death instead, as I hope she can. I take a deep breath and try to quell the growing fear in my voice.

"Hogan sank four birdies in seven holes." My voice breaks, and a fat tear rolls down my cheek. "He was a terrible putter. You know that. Ever since the accident, he had such a tough time on the green. But this time, in 1967, he stood over his last birdie putt, drew back, and sank it. He came home in 30 and carded a 66. Don't you remember?" My voice trails to a whisper.

Her fingers tighten around Jones's golf ball, and she caresses it for a moment before placing it back in my own worn hands.

"Oh, Daddy," she exclaims, laughing. "Didn't you learn *anything* at West Wind?"

At that moment, her eyes gleam just as Jones's did, with a wisdom that always seems to elude me.

"It's your destiny to teach," she says, "and it's my game to win or lose."

A Word from the Author

The Masters of the Spirit is, of course, a work of fiction. But wherever possible, I've included actual historical details. At the 1972 PGA Championship, Gary Player did indeed hit a miracle shot over a willow tree to the green on the sixteenth hole at Oakland Hills, and a spectator did throw a cup of ice at him as a way of protesting South Africa's then apartheid government. The gallery's initial dislike of Jack Nicklaus is well documented, as is the cruel taunting he endured. When Byron Nelson was a young tour player, he did have only two pairs of socks, knitted for him by his wife, Louise, and he washed one pair out each night in order to have a clean pair to wear in the morning.

I hope you've enjoyed the rich history of the game that I've woven into Zachary's story. The spiritual lessons of each champion are mine, and most of the words the champions say were spoken only in my own imagination. However, I believe that a person's life stands as a record of his or her spiritual beliefs, and in this regard, I think I've accurately described each of the champions' secrets.

I learned the eight spiritual principles of this book as a child, and I continue to practice them now as an adult. They were a gift to me from the real Zachary—my father—who taught me to see the course of life as a place of love and destiny. It's my wish that by reading about Zachary's journey at West Wind, you'll learn to see life through his eyes.

I welcome you to share your thoughts and comments with me.

Anne Kinsman Fisher
P.O. Box 10024
Savannah, Georgia 31401

E-mail: GolfWriter@aol.com

Source Material
and Suggested Readings

ALTHOUGH VERY LITTLE of the dialogue in this book is historical—fewer than one hundred words per golfer—you may find it of
interest to go "back to the source." I know I did. Like Zachary, I
found that biographies of the golfing greats gave me a special window into their souls. I can particularly recommend these books,
which I used during my research:

The Walter Hagen Story by Walter Hagen (Simon and Schuster, 1956)

Fit for Golf by Gary Player (Simon and Schuster, 1995)

Golfer's Gold by Tony Lema (Little, Brown, 1964)

Golf My Way by Jack Nicklaus (Simon and Schuster, 1974)

The Little Black Book by Byron Nelson (Summit Publishing, 1995)

Byron Nelson: How I Played the Game by Byron Nelson (Taylor
Publishing, 1993)

Arnold Palmer: A Personal Journey by Thomas Hauser
(CollinsPublishersSanFrancisco, 1994)

*A Hard Case from Texas: A Historical Documentary of the Life and Times
of Ben Hogan* (Pinehurst Golf Films, Inc., 1994)

The Hogan Mystique by Jules Alexander (The American Golfer, 1994)

The Life and Times of Bobby Jones by Sidney Matthew (Sleeping Bear
Press, 1995)

Down the Fairway by Bobby Jones and O. B. Keeler (The Classics of
Golf, Ailsa, Inc., 1985)